AN ILLUSTRATED HISTORY

BRITISH WATERWAYS

D. D. GLADWIN

SPURBOOKS LIMITED

Published by Spurbooks Ltd
6 Parade Court Bourne End Buckinghamshire

© D. D. Gladwin 1977

ISBN 0 904978 28 1

Designed and Produced by
Mechanick Exercises, London

Typesetting by Inforum Ltd, Portsmouth
Printed in Great Britain by Chapel River Press, Andover
Bound by Mansell, Witham.

CONTENTS

ACKNOWLEDGEMENTS

No book worthy of its readers could be written without the ideas, thoughts and assistance of many people. It is a pleasure to acknowledge just how much I owe to those of whom, alas, only a few can be mentioned by name; to those who remain anonymous my thanks are no less sincere.

*   *   *

Hugh & Mary Barker; Mike Black; the late George Bate, B.E.M.; J.K. Ebble-white; W.K.V. Gale; Phil Garrett; J. Hill; F.W. Jones of Solihull and F. Power of Dudley (photographic prints); Sir John & Lady Knill; Tony Pierce; Stan Turner; Frank White; Phil White.

*   *   *

L.J. Dalby (Kennet & Avon Trust); Miss Sheila Doeg (British Waterways Board); Martyn Denney (Narrow Boat Trust); L.A. 'Teddy' Edwards (East Anglian Waterways Association); Tom & Jean Henshaw (Ashby Canal Association); The Secretary and staff of the Inland Waterways Association; Mrs. Sheila Nix (Pocklington Canal Amenity Society); Mrs. Estelle Huxley (of the Publishers' office); M.W. Richards, Photographic Librarian, Royal Society for the Protection of Birds; Bob Shopland, Editor, *Waterways World*; P.L. Smith (Barge & Canal Development Association).

*   *   *

The Assistant Secretary, Institution of Mining Engineers; Miss B. Barley, F.L.A. and staff, Worcester & Hereford County Library Service; Miss D. McCulla, F.L.A. and staff, Local Studies Department, Birmingham Public Libraries; The Archivist and staff, Public Record Office, London; Librarians, Archivists and staffs of many libraries and record offices, particularly Bath, Bradford, Bristol, Chesterfield, Dudley, Gloucester, Newbury, Swindon and Taunton.

*   *   *

Our thanks must be expressed to the following authors and publishers for permission to reproduce copyright material:
The Birmingham Canal Society's *Yearbook;* British Waterways Board (*Lock & Quay, Waterways, The Facts about the Waterways*); Gladwin D.D. & J.M. *Canals of the Welsh Valleys,* published by the Oakwood Press, 1975; Rev. J. Skinner, *Journal of a Somerset Rector 1803-1834,* published by the Kingsmead Press, Bath; William T.S. *River Navigation in England 1600-1750,* Frank Cass & Co. Ltd. 1964; E. Wilson, *The Ellesmere and Llangollen Canal,* published by Phillimore & Co. Ltd; H.M.S.O. *Handbook on Canals* and the Inland Waterways Association Ltd for extracts from Bulletins and other documents.

*   *   *

My greatest debt is to my wife who has to cope with my natural untidiness — imagine a living-room with 900 photographs spread over every available inch — while acting as my secretary and general factotum.

1

THE VENTURESOME AGE

The story of artificial waterways in Britain goes back to, and possibly beyond, Roman times. Unfortunately, as any schoolchild knows, although the Romans were extremely good at recording when Antony was passing the time with Cleopatra, or Caesar knocking the Brits about, copies of their toll registers, *'instructions to lock-keepers and boatmen',* are a little sparse and therefore until well after Roman times just which navigations were in use, what was carried and by whom, is largely conjectural. Certainly they had an extensive network of artificial cuts in use in the wet 'fens' of Cambridgeshire and Lincolnshire, which in all probability gave them reasonably fast transport between the arable lands of Cambridgeshire and the cities of Lincoln and York.

Lincoln was, of course, the main 'stepping stone' for Roman advances through England and, later, a vital staging post, which meant that a population well in excess of the normal would give rise to some shortages of food, thus forcing the importation of grain. It was, therefore, perfectly logical for the Romans, who were well versed in the use of water carriage, to cut channels suitable for barges, rather than, initially at least, to undertake the vastly more expensive and labour-consuming task of building roads.

The Caer Dyke, as an example of their work, was probably about 40 miles long and by incorporating other streams and rivers ran from the Nene River near Peterborough to the Witham about three miles below Lincoln. Its supposed cross section, 8' (2.4 m) deep, 30' (9 m) wide at the bottom and 50' (15 m) wide at the top, compares well with the standard 'narrow' canals of the 18th and 19th centuries. It was probably cut around AD 50 or 60, at a time when the Romans were expanding their territory, but the local finds of coins, plus the dating of rubbish used to infill the channel leads to the belief that it went out of use as a means of navigation at the end of the second century A.D., when the greater availability of labour, and lessened numbers of soldiers may have meant greater use of local land for grain growing and decreased demand. By 1815 this waterway was described as "now almost wholly filled up" and today is in places almost indiscernible.

In 1675 a pamphlet 'Avona' expressed quaintly, a truism that, for all the growth of road traffic, is applicable even today: "... *there is more advantage to those places, which being seated far within the Land do enjoy the benefit of Commerce by Sea, by*

Lincoln Cathedral from Brayford Mere, which links the River Witham to the Fossdyke Canal

some Navigable River, than to those Port-Towns which are seated in some Creeke or Bay only, and are (as I may call it) Land-lock'd, having no passage up into the Land but by Carriages; . . . For such places, though the Sea brings in commodities to them, yet they can neither without great change convey those commodities higher up into the Land, nor, without the like charge, receive the Inn-land commodities to export again.

As a digression the author also mentions that *"Scurvies, Quartanes and other lingring Diseases"* were more common near the sea, than inland where the air is *"more sprightly and stirring"*; we now believe the converse to be true, having chemically and physically despoiled both land and air.

Whether artificial navigations are, or were, part of this despoliation is a moot point; no doubt when the 'navvies' were at work it was thought so. The claim was also advanced as early as 1350, when a plea for improving the navigation of the Trent was rejected on the grounds that it would *"obstruct the free passage of His Majesties subjects"* and be *"unsightly in his eyes"*. Simultaneously and contrarily Edward III passed a Bill relating to mills, weirs and other obstructions on inland navigations which were to be *"utterly pulled down"*. It was obviously of little avail, for in 1371 the penalty was increased!

During the reign of Henry VIII (1509-1547) the Stour in Kent was made navigable to Canterbury but Daniel Defoe writing in 1724 states that *"the person who undertook it, not meeting with encouragement and failing in the carrying it on, the locks and sluices are all run to decay, and the citizens are oblig'd to fetch all their heavy goods, either from Fordwich, three miles off, or from Whitstable seven miles off"*, apparently a matter of some hardship.

Boat passage up the Stour from Fordwich was by means of two 'flash' locks, the precursors of the locks of today. Basically, although their form varied greatly, they consisted of two wooden or masonry piers which constricted the flow of water. The gap was closed by either vertical planks and posts (paddles and rymers) or a single 'watergate' opened and closed by means of a winch on the bank. When the movable section was closed the water level slowly rose allowing a downhill barge to get over the shallows until it reached the lock. The gate or rymers swung or lifted, the resulting 'flash' would, with luck, take it down to the next lock. A barge working upstream would be dragged through the hole, against the flow of the water, either by winch, horses or *"a prodijious quantity of men, about 60 in number"*. The original scheme would have called for the lock to be set in advance, thus reducing delays, but water-mill owners relied upon a free-flowing stream and, by virtue of being there first and the fact that Milord Land-owner needed flour more than he needed the barge, the miller more or less decided when the barge might proceed — a vexing procedure leading to delays, not of hours but sometimes days. In a report made by a Committee appointed by Parliament to enquire into the state of the Thames as late as 1793 the following passage appears: *"Barges are frequently detained in Summer from Want of Water Five or Six days, and he [the Engineer] has known them a Fortnight; that flashing is much used on the*

Caer Dyke at Peakirk

The Welland Navigation in the Fens

River, which is a very abominable Practice, because after the Flash is drawn, and the Lock shut in again, it leaves the River almost dry for Twenty-four Hours, insomuch that he has walked over the Channel of the River at Marlow, without wetting his Feet; and Barges navigating upwards are stopped for many Hours".

At the time, it was said, Thames barges could not make more than *"Eight or Nine Trips a Year between Reading and London"* but that their carriage rate was only 50p per ton compared with *"Land Carriage of Goods [which] is Thirty-three Shillings and Four Pence per Ton [£1.67]"*. The City of London Clerk of Works was asked what the cure for the bargemasters' problems was and replied *". . . that he knows of no other Method by which the River could be effectually improved, so as to give Three Feet Ten Inches of Water at all Times, but by making of Pound Locks, which (as there is 36 Feet Fall) he apprehends would require Nine Locks from Staines to Richmond; but a Canal Navigation would be preferable to the River with such Pound Locks"*.

Among other problems involved in 'flashing' on this, our greatest river, and indeed most others, were the lack of a towpath *"it having been washed away by the Flood"*; the excessive animal power required *"Twelve to Sixteen Horses are required upon the River"*; the expence of 'hawling'- or tow-ropes *"One of £13 Value being worn out in about Three Voyages"* and general obstructions by landowners — when a proposal for a new towpath was made it had to be dropped, *"the Question of some*

Lincoln from the waterside, 1973

Willow Trees" being the deciding factor. Poor workmanship was an inherent weakness, it is axiomatic that a free-flowing river liable to flood in winter and drying-out in summer requires stronger works than a canal, but rarely were they so. Robert Mylne, an engineer called in to survey the Thames from Lechlade to Whitchurch, was scathing about the workmanship at Osney Lock, various parts having collapsed *"on Account of the improper Manner of laying the Foundation"*; the man who built the lock being a Mr. Daniel Harris, *"Gaol Keeper at Oxford"*, who, not unsurprisingly, *"had never been employed in such Works before"*!

It would have been as well, perhaps, if he had been gaoler to the criminals responsible when it was reported in 1684 by John Aubrey that Captain Andrew Yarranton had *"dyed in London about March last"*, the cause of his death being *"a Beating and throwne into a Tub of Water"*. Assuming it was the same man, this was doubly unfortunate for him, as he had been for some twenty years previous to this engaged in endeavouring to persuade anyone with money that river navigations were vital to the future of England.

In 1677 Yarranton had produced a well-reasoned pamphlet suggesting, *inter alia*, that virtually all imported items could be made here, particularly linen and iron. Of the former he claimed *". . . we should prevent at least two millions of money a year from being sent out of the Land for Linen Cloth, and keep our people at home who now go*

15

Newark Lock, River Trent

beyond the Seas for want of employment here", and for iron he projected "making Navigable" the River Stour in Warwickshire, having obtained an Act of Parliament
in 1662 to enable him to do so: *"Upon which I fell on, and made it compleatly navigable
from Sturbridge to Kederminster; and carried down many hundred Tuns of Coales, and laid out
near one thousand pounds, and then it was obstructed for Want of Money, which by Contract
was to be paid".* Shortly, probably no more than a decade after this, *"a sudden and violent flood. . . . destroyed all the works".*

Among the other projects of Yarranton was a small iron and tin plating works
in a then remote valley in Worcestershire between Astley and Shrawley. The
iron slag was obtained from Worcester fairly easily via the River Severn, but getting it the last few miles, a packhorse load at a time was somewhat tedious and
difficult, and therefore, in the 1650s, he made the Dick Brook navigable with
two flash locks in its three-quarter mile (1.2 km) length. Although relics of the
navigation are still plentiful, nevertheless the active life of the ironworks and its
navigation was probably not more than twenty years. Instead of tin, iron, coal,
wood, slag-heaps and men, now (usually) there are only teasel, figwort, fox-
glove, burdock, elder plants and birds.

The story of Exeter, the River Exe and the Exeter Canal is one open to many

Ancient Bridge, St. Ives, Hunts.

interpretations, depending on whose documents are studied. Basically it seems that the River Exe was once navigable to the city walls, but the Mayor of Exeter and the Earl of Devon had a rather daft argument over *"which of their purveyors should be first served with a dish of fish in the market"* and the Earl somewhat spitefully, but also profitably, *"built weirs with timber, sand, etc. which choaked up the river and entirely ruined the navigation"*. The result was that Topsham village, of which the Earl was sole landowner, *"suddenly acquired the whole maritime trade of the river"*. Other sources claim it was Isabella de Fortibus, Countess of Devon, who had the weir built — a possibility, as even today the village name Countess Wear remains; but either way the upshot was that by the end of the 13th century Topsham received all the trade, on-carriage being by cart, or pack-horse.

In 1563 John Trew of Glamorganshire, *"Gentleman"*, was paid by the Corporation of Exeter to build a new canal 1.75 miles (2.8 km) long, parallel to the river and incorporating three 'pound' locks; generally accepted to be the first in England, although, like early navigation locks in Holland, single gates wound round by a windlass were used instead of today's counterbalanced pairs of gates. These works took about two years, but while probably well built for the period, maintenance must have been poor — possibly due in part to the fraças which then occurred between the King and the Puritans.

Between 1665 and 1670 another engineer, Richard Hurd, extensively repaired the old waterway and carried the artificial channel upstream for a further half-a-mile, theoretically re-opening the navigation to Exeter. Whether this was so or not, by 1698 when Celia Fiennes cast her watchful eyes over the area, navigation was apparently impossible. After describing the millowners' habits *". . . they have made severall bays or wires* [weirs] *which casts the water into many channells for the conveniencys of turning all their mills"* and those of the local fishermen who sat or stood patiently by the mill-races *". . . those wires* [weirs] *makes great falls into the water it comes with great violence, here they catch the salmon as they leap, with speares"*, she states that *". . . they are attempting to make* [the river] *navigeable to the town which will be of mighty advantage to have shipps come up close to the town to take in their serges, which now they are forced to send to Topsham on horses by land which is about 4 mile by land"*.

On the whole the Burgesses did not do too well by their canal, for in 1698 they arranged with one William Bayley (or Baily) that he should complete the navigation to Exeter at a cost of *"5 or 6000£"*, but he decamped the following year (complete with the city's money) and they then had to employ Daniel Dunnell at the handsome wage of £3 per week, to complete the waterway by 1701 at an estimated cost of £7,000. Interestingly, the original specification of the sea-lock still remains, and after stating a *"plate of Cast Iron"* was run around the *"Upper Apron"* of the lock continues *". . . each and every of the Said Gates shall have One Wheele of Brasse att the Outer Corner thereof, which wheele shall Turne upon the said plate of Iron and keepe the said Gates from Dragging"*; length was to be 350′ (107 m), width through gates 26′ (8 m) and for draught there was to be *"Fowerteenth Foot depth of water upon the Apron* [cill]*"*. The lock was not rectangular however, but semi-circular for the middle *"Two hundred Foot"* (61 m) were to be not less than *"Seaventy and Five Foot"* (23 m) in breadth, thus enabling the lock chamber to act as a mini-dock.

So far we have seen the power of the landowner (the Earl and Countess of Devon), the 'one-man-band' engineer (Yarranton), the city (Exeter) and it is as well to recap on precisely what one or any group of promotors could or could not do.

In Scotland, at Upper Largo, there is a fine old church, consecrated on 17th July 1243 by David de Bernham, a striking feature of which is the much admired spire, a gift of Peter Black who bought the estate of Largo from the Wood family in 1611. Sir Andrew Wood is reputed, locally at least, to have had a canal made from Largo House to the church and made his church-going in a barge which had English prisoners as its motive power!

A little later, in the more lawful days of Good King Charles, rivers were made

The Thames Barge c.1800

navigable under 'letters patent', being a grant direct from the King, who received some monetary benefit, to the man prepared, literally, to stick his neck out. These men were known, appositely, as 'undertakers'. For example Arnold Spencer was, on 3rd January 1628, granted the exclusive right *"to cut and make locks, sluices, bridges, cuts, dams and other inventions not repugnant to our laws, for the making of rivers and streams navigable in all places convenient within our realm of England, dominion of Wales and town of Berwick"*, taking the profits but paying an annual rental of £5 per river. Had it been strictly adhered to, this 'patent' would have been, to other aspiring engineers, excessively restrictive. Fortunately there was more than one 'letter patent' granted by the King; given a good cause and enough cash any optimist could try his luck. The whole system was grossly inefficient and as long ago as 1655 one Francis Matthew, pre-dating Karl Marx, protested bitterly that *"Such great and publick Works, are not to be attempted by private men, or any particular Corporations; But most fit it were that the State itself should be the sole Undertaker, performing all at its own proper charge"*.

Initially the over-riding control of rivers lay in the hands of the 'Commissioners of Sewers' but it was apparent that their responsibility began and ended with land draining and flood prevention. This is not to say that they, by cleansing a river, would not help boats going about their business but they were specifically disbarred from making new navigations and trying *"Inventions at the charge of the Country"*.

19

The Medway was in 1600 the scene of a pitched verbal battle between the Commissioners of Sewers (indirectly supporting the navigation and worried about floods) and the owners of fish weirs or kiddles at various villages. The pro-navigation side claimed that land carriage ruined roads and the removal of weirs only made fish a little "subtiller". The fishermen listed the usual moans about bargees stealing, breaking down fences, etc., and stated that such works as locks caused the decay of husbandry and ruined road-hauliers. Although the Commissioners won it was solely on the grounds that the fish weirs choked the *"cleansing flow of water"*.

The whole question of river navigation is still complicated by the fact that everything belongs either to the Crown, the State or the private individual, but demarkation limits are often difficult to establish. In the case of non-tidal rivers ownership is vested in the riparian owners (i.e. those who own the lands adjacent to the river) but tidal rivers *". . . so far as the Sea flows and ebbs are a Royal stream, and the Fishing belongs to the Crown"* but are, however, for navigation purposes free and common to all.

With the coming of the Commonwealth, it was decreed that the right to charge for navigation after improvements had been carried out (and, *inter alia*, the right to trespass in order to carry out the works) should be granted not by the Crown, but by Parliament, and 'Letters Patent' ceased to be issued. The right to actually navigate canals and rivers, hitherto inalienable, was removed by the 1968 Transport Act, Section 105(S).

At this juncture, since it has great bearing on the age of canal building, it is as well to clarify by example the procedure carried out in getting authority from Parliament to cut or modify the channel of a canal or river.

On 9th January 1700 a petition was presented to Parliament which read in part *"That the making and keeping navigable the River Lark, alias Burn, would be a means to employ great numbers of poor People and improve Trade and Commerce, by affording an easy Communication between Bury and Lynn Regis by Water, and furnishing the Petitioners, and Places adjacent with Fuel, and Sea Coal, from Lynn, and other merchantable Commodities"*.

On 24th January, Mr. J. Harvey, the Agent, presented to the House of Commons a Bill for making the River Lark navigable and they resolved *"That the Bill be read To-morrow Morning"*, which it duly was and simultaneously a petition was presented by the Mayor and Burgesses of Kings Lynn, claiming that making the river navigable would seem to be a *"Work of general Advantage to the Country; and a particular Increase of the Shipping, Trade and Navigation of the said Port; And praying, that the House will give all suitable Encouragement to the Undertakers of so good a Work"*.

On 31st January, the Bill was read a second time and referred to an House of Commons committee consisting of 42 gentlemen, knights and baronets plus *"all that serve for the Counties of Norfolk, Suffolk and Cambridge"*, the whole crew being ordered *"to meet this Afternoon, at Four a Clock in the Speaker's Chambers"*.

Another petition was added to the heap of paper, this one from *"the Capital Bur-*

gesses of Wisbech, the Justices of Peace, Deputy Lieutenant and other chief Inhabitants and Freeholders" of no less than twelve towns — albeit one had a total population of 32! This petition stated that "... the said Towns, and Country adjacent, for above Ten Miles Compass, for the most Part, consists of Pasture, Marsh, and Fen Lands, the Produce whereof is mostly for feeding of Cattle, Butter, Cheese and Summer Crops of Oats; and they being supplied with wheat, Rye, and Malt, from other Countries, especially from St. Edmund's-bury, and the Parts of Suffolk adjoining, by way of Return, for want of Navigation to and from thence, their interchangeable Supply becomes very chargeable, and, in Winter Time, by Badness of the Way, impracticable", and hoped the Bill would be passed.

On 28th February, "Mr. Hervey [sic] reported from the Committee, to whom the Bill for making the River Lark, alias Burne, navigable, was committed, That they had to make several Amendments to the Bill; which they had directed him to report to the House, which he read in his Place; and afterwards delivered in at the Clerk's Table". After a very complicated internal procedure, in amended form it received its first and second readings that day, the third on 4th March and trundled off to the House of Lords to obtain their "concurrence".

The Lords waffled a bit but after some minor amendments, including one allowing landowners to carry manure free of toll, they passed it on the 14th March. Back to the Commons, where they agreed to the amendments on 19th March, the whole plan becoming law on 11th April 1700.

Unfortunately, at this time the power to "make and maintain" the waterway

Pleasure Boat Inn, Hickling Broad

was vested in the hands of 'Commissioners' the first batch being appointed, or at least agreed to, by Parliament. There was no way of breaking into this, the original closed shop, unless the Commissioners cared to vote someone else in, which they rarely did, and as age, illness or neglect took their toll so the administration of the waterway ran down. By 1805 this had happened to the Lark, and *"great inconvenience arose from the neglect of the commissioners in not filling up vacancies"*, so much so that the waterway had fallen into total disrepair.

However, this relatively isolated river navigation fell outside the mainstream of later stillwater navigation plans. Of much greater importance was an Act obtained by Scroop, the second Duke of Bridgewater, in 1737 — an Act to make a navigation from Worsley Mill to the River Irwell utilising the Worsley Brook, but it was not, due to *"the degree of supineness exhibited by the original undertakers"*, until his son was jilted and retired to his estates in dudgeon that anything happened.

As a youth our Duke of Bridgewater had travelled on the 'Grand Tour' of Europe from March 1752 to September 1755, undertaken by most in his position as a part of the educational process and during which tour he inspected various waterways. No doubt seeking to improve his family fortunes and having time on his hands it was logical for him to consider improving access to his coalfields at Worsley. Described variously as *"the Most Noble Francis, Duke of Bridgewater"* and as *"The Father of British Inland Navigation"*, the Duke could not have avoided seeing the work of a great pioneer engineer, Henry Berry, on the nearby St. Helen's Canal, but — else how history might have been changed — Berry, by now in charge of modifications to the River Weaver, was under a cloud in 1759. In the Spring of that year floodwater on the river breached an artificial cut and the resultant collapse of nearby salt workings caused a lock to be destroyed. When, later, a weir for which Berry, as engineer in charge, was responsible, was washed away, his employers considered it *"imprudent to employ him any longer"* and he retired from the scene of canal building. His going left the door open for the man who was most to influence the shape of our waterways — James Brindley.

2
THE HEROIC AGE

The heroic age of waterways began in 1759 with the commencement of work on the Duke of Bridgewater's canal and might reasonably be said to have ended with the sale or lease of over one third of the total navigable mileage to the upstart railways. In between, like a regiment, canals saw many campaigns fought, some won easy victories, some won against overwhelming odds, and a few lost — even some that were won proved to have been pyrrhic victories, the company bankrupting themselves in the process of getting their canal partly or wholly open.

To continue the military simile, the ranks of the men involved included the private, a navvy with *"the industry of bees, or labour of ants"*; the non-commissioned officer, perhaps a carpenter or blacksmith, "cunning men" while a junior officer might equate to the resident engineer, a gentleman who should *"possess a considerable degree of mathematical knowledge, have studied the elements of most of the sciences"* [and] *"particularly excel in an acquaintance with the various branches of mechanics"*. Senior staff officers were the consulting engineers — Telford, *"a man more heartily to be liked, more worthy to be esteemed and admired"*, Rennie who *"declined the offer of a knighthood from the Prince Regent"* or Brindley *"enthusiastically attached to his profession"*.

Behind the lines lay the administration corps, a veritable battery of clerks, accountants, treasurers, time-keepers and their quill-pushing ilk.

Further behind, at base, were the leading promotors and shareholders, generally content to give orders, and unwilling to listen to excuses whatever the cause. There were exceptions. That man of peace John Thomas, a Quaker, started life as a grocer and, taking a great interest in *"the best constructed canal in Europe"* — the Kennet & Avon — for ever earned the respect of his employees when, in 1813, he stated that it was a disgrace that such a canal should pay its lock-keepers too little to live on.

The basis of a canal campaign was simple enough and, generally, was based on honest, if sometimes inefficient, surveys of available traffic between two or more points. Early waterways had a solid foundation with guaranteed trade, thus the Trent & Mersey canal was to carry clay and other potter's materials in to their factories and to disperse the finished products to the widest available markets. This is an over simplification, but was a tangible operation. The factory existed. It could expand given a better supply of coal, potter's clay and water. Breakages, when the goods were carried by pack-horse or stage-wagon, both raised the price to the dealer and stultified expansion. These would be reduced to infinitesimal proportions.

But later canals, stripped of the promotors flim-flam, offered more vague traffics. *"The means for conveyance of goods, market garden produce, corn, merchandise, etc. to and from the metropolis being limited, expensive, and of a very inadequate description, the necessity for a Canal to carry this traffic . . . is seriously felt"*. The cost of this one, the Romford, was to be £80,000. With annual expenses estimated at £13,400 and a theoretical income at best of £16,000 no better dividend than 3¼% could be offered — and this was nebulous.

Just how woefully inaccurate a quotation could be may be typified by the saga of the Croydon Canal. In 1799 the cost of building it was estimated at £25,000 and great promises were made of the traffic that would be carried. By the opening date, 1809, the outlay had been £127,000, and with such a vastly inflated cost, the shareholders were lucky when they received a dividend of 1%. With hindsight it is obvious they would have done better to have taken note of an unbiased engineer, John Rennie, when in 1800 he shrewdly warned them, *"If the Lock Canal is adopted, I do not apprehend there will ever be more than five boats pass up and down daily on the average"* and kept their money elsewhere!

The Grosvenor Canal, on the other hand, suffered from ill-advised promotors' haste. The annual report of 1826 shows how over-riding their engineer backfired on costs. The basic estimate for cutting the channels, wharfs, stop lock and other components of a navigation, was a total of £26,500. Various changes to the original plan, including making the canal wider, added an extra £2,228. However, the waterway was brought into use before completion, and costs accelerated solely because of this — a fairly hefty amount being detailed as *"To putting a pipe through the Bank at the head of the Layby for the use of the Trade before the Canal was completed. . . . To repairing the Basin and Wharf Walls injured by the admission of the Trade into the Basin before the Coping was set"*. The overall total cost was £31,713 — or an increase on estimate of about 20%.

The common urge activating all promotors of waterways and their shareholders was one of making money. But, regard, this was at a time when the pound in your pocket should be worth a pound tomorrow, or in one, five or even twenty-five years time. Given that they had not the distractions of today — the pretty junk sold through shops — if careful enough to save a pound when they could and to cautiously invest it that pound would bring in a steady 4%; £1,000 so invested was enough to keep a wise couple for a year! But when the Duke of Bridgewater was found to be making a seemingly vast income from his waterway, perhaps not realising just how special his circumstances were, perfectly ordinary, decent, folk suddenly rushed to withdraw, borrow, mortgage or otherwise acquire cash in the hope that their 4% would become 104%! Alas for the frailty of man's plans!

Perhaps many waterways that might have paid a moderate dividend could have been completed if the engineer had done his job properly. Too many did not and the resulting delay brought the waterway, its personnel and their dreams, face to face with the inflation caused by the Napoleonic wars.

As there were commenced at one time and another some 200 navigations, we have to narrow the field. Taking lists of stocks and shares dated 1833 we have the following canals that were, at that time, successful:

Canal	Nominal Face Value	Selling Price
Barnsley	£160	£290
Birmingham	£ 17.50	£233.50
Coventry	£100	£600
Cromford	£100	£300
Erewash	£100	£705
Staffs & Worcs	£140	£610
Trent & Mersey	£ 50	£640

Amongst those surviving, if only by their fingernails, were the:

Basingstoke	£100	£5.25
Wilts & Berks	£100	£5.50
Grand Western	£100	£ 21
Kennet & Avon	£100	£ 27
Kensington	£100	£ 10

Dying, if not moribund, came others:

Carlisle	£ 50	£1
Croydon	£100	£1
Thames & Medway	£100	£1

The greatest 'if' in the canal world is 'if the Napoleonic wars had not occurred how much success could other waterways have had?' The 'other' includes those that were unlucky enough to overrun the period of financial instability of 1803 to 1815; the most successful waterways included the:

Birmingham	commenced	1768	completed	1772
Coventry	,,	1768	,,	1790
Staffs & Worcs	,,	1766	,,	1772
Trent & Mersey	,,	1766	,,	1777

Wedgwood's Etruria Works, Trent & Mersey Canal, 125 years ago

Whether the shareholders were shrewd, lucky or bold, the fact remains these waterways were incredibly good investments but it is advantageous to view the other causes for the difference in the outcomes of the various fortunes of canals, which, in essence, come down to human frailty.

Having thought that it would be a good idea to build a canal and having gathered a few like-minded colleagues who were willing to put up the few hundred pounds required to cover basic costs, our promotor would find an engineer to carry out a cursory survey of the proposed route. If this engineer were Brindley or Telford the chances were that he would, because of pressure of work, depute this to one of his pupils, merely checking that the basic facts were right. If one of the lesser breed of contractors-cum-engineers, the work would be carried out skimpily and vast optimism expressed. The good engineers had too much work, the lesser wanted all they could get.

Assuming that the route was, or was believed to be, feasible, a prospectus would be issued, putting the best face on prospects and ignoring the nastier bits of the engineer's report. No prospectus was ever backward in its claims but the Regent's Canal, London, was overweeningly self-confident:

"The Advantages of such a Canal to the Public are incalculable, but amongst the most prominent is the supplying the whole of the North Side of the Metropolis, for an Extent of

26

Eight Miles with Water Carriage. It will be another Thames at the Back of the Northern Parts of the Town, affording the like Advantages of Commerce and Communication, as the River Thames itself. . . . Considering but for a Moment the vast Trade carrying on, and the numerous Manufactories in the very populous Parts of London, upon the North of the River Thames, extending for several Miles, and even far North of the Line of the intended Canal, the Mind must be at once impressed with an Immensity of Traffic that must necessarily be carried upon it when executed, but cannot possibly contemplate the Magnitude and Extent of it".

Shares would then be put on the market, requiring a deposit of 5% (5p in the £1) or so, to be put on the table when names were put down. Having this amount in their pockets the promotors would normally go back to their chosen engineer (although sometimes having doubts they ditched him and found another). Once again the fortunes of the dairymaid and the stockbroker hung in the balance, for while some work would be farmed out, the conscientious man — Brindley, Telford, Rennie, Jessop — would ride the proposed route not once but many times, until they were entirely satisfied that the line specified was the best available.

James Brindley indeed, was so overworked that he took risks with his health, finally taking one too many when riding along the proposed Caldon canal. Admittedly he had undiagnosed diabetes, but getting soaked to the skin was not conducive to good health. One of the most remarkable tributes was written by his friend Josiah Wedgwood to Thomas Bentley on 26th September 1772. Reading it shows how much admiration there was for this man, especially as this was a

Grosvenor Canal 1826-1920

private letter. *". . . the present illness, which I fear will deprive us of a valuable friend, and the world of one of the greatest Genius's who seldom live to see justice done to their singular abilities, but must trust to future ages for that tribute of praise and fair fame they so greatly merit from their fellow mortals. Poor Mrs. Brindley is inconsolable . . .".* Wedgwood wrote in the same vein to Doctor Darwin, who four days later replied: *"Your letter . . . gave me most sincere grief about Mr. Brindley, whom I have always esteem'd to be a great Genius and whose loss is truly a public one. I don't believe he has left his equal. I think the various Navigations should erect him a monument in Westminster Abbey. . . ."*

At the other end of the scale came James Hollinsworth (who succeeded his father as engineer of the Crinan canal in 1811), being dismissed for incompetence in January 1812, and Joseph Hill (engineer of the Southampton & Salisbury canal debacle) of whose standard of work it was said by another engineer, *". . . I have never had through my hands a work where less attention seems to have been paid to the Proprietors' interest. . . ."*

Having chosen an engineer the proprietors were not to know that his work might not be up to standard, but took his report plus statements of expected traffic, lists of subscribers, etc., and applied for an Act of Parliament in order to commence work. With luck this application might go smoothly, especially if a few palms were greased, but should the line threaten to upset the game converts, grouse, partridge or deer of one of the great landowners then some 'accommodation' would have to be reached; for they were the real powers in the land. The engineer would then have to alter the proposed line, ensuring that in the process the canal remained invisible from m'Lord's house and did not draw water from his streams. The difficulty here lay in that all this was done in a hurry, as a year's delay could well be fatal to the whole project and the expense unendurable. In such circumstances even the great Thomas Telford could fail. Shelmore Bank on the Birmingham & Liverpool Junction canal (now the main line of the Shropshire Union canal) was built as the result of the petty intransigence of such a landowner who insisted the line should be diverted. Too late, when Parliamentary plans had been passed, it was found that the land was marl, a belated discovery that cost the company both money and time, delaying the opening of the waterway by some three years, and bringing them face to face with railway competition. It seems a pity that so magnificent a man, the orphaned son of a crofter, who had worked his way up to face an honourable retirement should spend his last days deaf, doubted and disturbed, at the whim of a bloated, self-satisfied, man who cared for nothing but his own trivial pleasures.

Even the lower echelons of landowners were not above this attitude, the poet Shelley writing of John Mitchell, appointed by Telford to be in charge of the works on the Caledonian canal notes that: *"Mr. Telford found him a working mason, who could scarcely read or write . . . [possessing] inflexible integrity, a fearless temper, and an indefatigable frame. . . . No fear or favour in the course of fifteen years have ever made him swerve from the fair performance of his duty, tho' the Lairds with whom he has to deal have*

28

Grosvenor Canal, the truncated remnants 1976

omitted no means to make him enter into their views, and do things, or leave them undone, as might suit their humour, or interest. They have attempted to cajole and to intimidate him, equally in vain. They have repeatedly preferred complaints against him in the hope of getting him removed from his office, and a more flexible person appointed in his stead; and they have not unfrequently threatened him with personal violence".

The act granted, the promotors would then make a further call on shares to enable work to commence. Little or no problems arose with the earlier canals but on the later ones mysterious things could happen. Mr. Smith of Bird Cottage, Puddletown, who had put his name down for 100 £10 shares might have moved, without leaving a forwarding address; Mrs. Smith of Little Twittering (50 x £10) turn out to have a widow's mite of 40p per week and S. Samson of Dogsteeth-on-Sea (25 shares) might prove to be the curate's canary! Too many would-be subscribers put their names down for shares merely as a speculation — sometimes it worked; on the Kennet & Avon canal subscribers immediately re-sold their shares and *"Many a common fellow having mustered £2 by loan or otherwise, found himself worth £5 or £50 soon after emerging from the tent".* Most times it did not, and when the demands for further payments came they could not be met, so the £2 or so per share already paid (and remember a labourer's wage was, in 1800, only 50p per week) was forfeit and the company could whistle for the rest.

At this juncture interested persons would 'plant' judiciously timed letters in

29

The Caldon Canal, Froghall tunnel

the local press or produce anonymous pamphlets extolling the virtues of the navigation. *"With Respect to Kendal, Lancaster, and perhaps Preston, it is now no longer a Question of Choice, but Necessity; — either they must put themselves on a Footing with their Southern Neighbours, or submit to a Decline of their Trade and Population, and a Decrease in the Value of their Land, as a natural and inevitable Consequence: In short, a Canal is now become as necessary an Appendage to a Manufacturing or Commercial Town as a Turnpike Road"*.

The capital may have been authorised at, say, £100,000; £73,000 promised but the final figure raised was only £58,000 as it was on the Dorset & Somerset canal. Such an occurrence, not uncommon, would lead to a rethink and the decision made either to truncate the route or to push on as far as possible in the hope that signs of work would induce a further inflow of funds. The great bugbear of either alternative was that the former required more expense in obtaining a further Act of Parliament and the latter could not always be undertaken because it was improbable that the extra funds would be obtained before the time limits laid down in the company's authorising Act expired.

The purchase price of land was another uncontrollable variable, for while Parliament authorised the actual purchase it did not stipulate a price to be paid. Obviously, if the inhabitants could be induced, by promises of cheap coal etc., to take a moderate price (some even gave the land!) all well and good, but if, say, a quarter-acre were vital for the immediate works a fantastic price (£1,000 or so) could be asked and, moreover, got. Should the area concerned be some distance from the contractor's present site and the matter, therefore, not pressingly urgent, the rather cumbersome and time consuming arbitration procedure would be used. Unfortunately, when the engineer drew up his first survey and estimate he could be happily vague, merely allowing a block sum of money (often about 10% of the total cost) for land and thus when the Reverend Snell of Hebblethwaite demanded £250 in lieu of the £16 offered for his acre it caused a flutter in the treasurer's dovecot; especially as the Reverend Bloggs of Bilth-waite-juxta-Hebblethwaite would feel he had underpriced *his* land (having provisionally accepted the £16) and raise his bill.

So our sum which should have purchased enough land for the whole length turns out to be only enough to cover half, or less.

During this time, while land negotiations were proceeding, contractors would be asked to tender for the next stage. Once again, as with most matters appertaining to canals, different men bred different command structures, and to recap our chain of authority we have:

SHAREHOLDERS
↓
DIRECTORS
↓
CONSULTING ENGINEER
↓
RESIDENT OR SITE ENGINEER

The possibilities open thereafter were:

1.   'Telford' style:

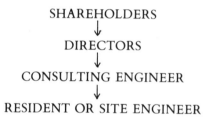

| CONSULTING ENGINEER AND RESIDENT ENGINEER | together would recommend and select main contractor who chose his own sub-contractors. |

2.   'Sheasby' style:

CONSULTING ENGINEER gives orders to RESIDENT ENGINEER who is main contractor and chooses his own sub-contractors.

3. 'Hill' style:

CONSULTING ENGINEER omits Site Engineer and selects many sub-contractors.

While in theory the engineer was disinterested, nevertheless, the choice of contractors was almost invariably based on his recommendations,

Where the engineer was of the Brindley/Telford class, contracts were given to men of known ability and in return these men would, realising the value of continued work, give all they could. Costs, too, could, due to demand, be high; Hazeldine, a protege of Telford, when manufacturing the iron work for Pontcysyllte Aqueduct built a new blast-furnace and ancillary works at Plas Kynaston and yet could still undercut the prices of the major ironmasters. Masonry, under the eagle eye of Telford, or his contractor Mitchell, as both were ex-masons, would be of the highest quality, with each stone properly squared and dowelled to its neighbour. The canal would be dug to the required dimensions — the contract for the Newport branch of the Shropshire Union canal required that the channel be *". . . at bottom 16' [5 m] and at the level of the top of the towing path 42' [13 m], the depth of water 5' [1.5 m], the height of the towing path and the top of the opposite bank 1' 6" [0.5 m] above the water surface; the breadth of the towing path in all cases. . . . to be 10' [3 m] except under the bridges"*, and it was stipulated that *"The whole of the Works to be completed in a Substantial and Proper manner to the satisfaction of MR. TELFORD, the Engineer in Chief, within two years after the signing of the Contract"*.

In the 'Sheasby' approach infinite variations were again possible for Josiah Clowes (Hereford & Gloucester canal), Thomas Sheasby (father and son, Swansea canal), Benjamin Outram (Peak Forest canal) and Thomas Dadford, Jnr. (Neath canal) to name only a few, had been contractors before they were engineers, changed hats at regular intervals and on at least one occasion three of them (the two Dadfords and Thomas Sheasby) banded together as contractors for the Glamorganshire canal, obviating the need for an engineer.

Unfortunately, whatever the causes — lack of experience, excess work, poor supervision, inflation or under capitalisation — workmanship was suspect. As maintenance men know all too well today, the geographical line of their canals is not always of the best and this contributed towards the fact that these engineer/contractors were prone to going bankrupt or being fired. This type of engineer, too, had the nasty habit of throwing up contracts when half-finished, which vexed shareholders greatly.

The third arrangement was typified at its worst by the antics of Joseph Hill on the Southampton & Salisbury canal when he appointed Edward Gee of Lockerley and Thomas Jenkins of Romsey (the latter recommended by the Kington,

Shropshire Union Canal, main line near Chester

Leominster & Stourport) as his main contractors. Trouble soon started, particularly with the Southampton tunnel and by the end of 1797 the difficulties with running sand and excess water were such that they were outside the experience of the local contractors. After disturbing reports by John Rennie, who had been called in, Joseph Hill was dismissed in 1799 for neglect and breach of agreement.

Fortunately, where the canal length was moderate, the area not short of labour and physical conditions reasonable, a local man could produce a well built canal without overmuch stress, perhaps the greatest part of George Leather's fame was that he saw to the building of one of the very few canals to be completed within the estimated price. This, the Pocklington, was considered *"likely to pay the adventurers"* on their speculation in a waterway that was designed *"to obtain coal, and lime for manure to Pocklington and its vicinity"* and to carry corn to the *"manufacturing districts"*.

May Upton was another competent, if not brilliant, general-purpose engineer who not only did without contractors when building the Wey & Arun Junction canal but was able to call upon the normal labour force employed by Lord Egremont, who owned much of the land through which the waterway ran, and could thus ensure costs were calculable.

If the contractor may be regarded as the Regimental Sergeant Major, sub-contractors the Sergeants, then under them came those vital men, Corporals, or in canal parlance, gangers. The work of a ganger, again by a form of tender, was to undertake a given number of cubic yards of the channel, rock or tunnel cutting (measured both by the waste removed and the end product) or to lay bricks, etc., according to his trade. In effect, this was the piece-work used today in many

33

Shropshire Union Canal, Welsh section, Pontcysyllte Aqueduct

trades, not one produced by a theoretical time and motion study but one established from the experience of the 'butty' or ganger himself elected by and responsible for half-a-dozen navvies. Another group might consist of two brick-layers, two hod-carriers, two mixers of mortar, plus a 'back-up' man whose rate, divided between them, was calculated per 'thousand of bricks' laid. The main contractor or the Company would be responsible for seeing all materials required were on hand. Tunnel blasting, another skilled trade, was often carried out by miners whose knowledge of land gave them a greater chance of quoting a realistic price, whether in sandstone or granite. Some £3,000 worth of gunpowder was used to blast through the 3,817 yards (3,490 m) of Sapperton Tunnel in 1783-1789 but for all that the best quotation was seven guineas (£7.35) per yard. All these small groups feared an eruption of greensand, springs, marl and other unexpected substances for not only were they hazarding their pockets — bad enough in the days before 'easy-come' dole — but also their lives. Casualties among navvies were, in the heroic age of canals, rarely reported, but death and maiming were as much their lot as that of the redcoat.

The cutting of Strood Tunnel on the Thames & Medway canal (1819-1824) accounted for a number of lives. The navvies suffered badly from accidents, not always of their own making, as sabotage of an ugly nature may have been responsible: *"Notwithstanding every possible precaution was taken to ascertain the soundness of the chalk [through which it was cut] and no expense was spared for timber for securing the workmen from injury . . . some serious accidents occurred, both from the fool-hardiness of the miners, and from wanton and wicked acts of others, in cutting the whin [winch] ropes nearly through, by which several were severely hurt, and one killed".* The commentator, rather candidly, added as an afterthought, *"In works of such magnitude it is scarcely possible to arrive at completion without occasional accidents".* By modern standards it is reasonable to suppose that the blame lay within the methods of working which were to say the least, hair-raising.

Sometimes the company's parsimony could easily lead to accidents — a prize system lay in the field of blasting. A hole was drilled in the rock by means of an oversize 'Rawlplug' tool, banged in with a sledgehammer, the explosive black powder rammed in by a 'punner' or rod, a fuse inserted and cottonwaste tamped in to plug the end. The fuse lit, everyone retired and the blast should loosen a few more cubic yards of rock. This operation was carried out by candlelight, up to 1500' (450 m) below the ground and was 'hairy' enough without two favourite economies. The first was the substitution of iron rods for copper when 'punning' the explosive. Iron, unlike copper, causes sparks off the rock and the result, all too often, was a premature explosion. One rod killed three men almost simultaneously at Standedge (Huddersfield Narrow canal) by passing through two and impaling the third! The other money-saver was the substitution of a trail of black powder for a fuse. Premature ignition again — working by candlelight and wearing hob-nailed boots, chances were high of this occurring — and a man or two lost his hands or was blinded. Small wonder the navvies had a reputation for hard working, hard drinking and hard living. Described as *"completely a class by themselves. . . . Possessed of all the daring recklessness of the Smuggler . . . their ferocious behaviour can only be equalled by the brutality of their language",* they carried out work that few men could do today, but then their staple diet was radically different from that of the 20th century, consisting primarily of beef, eggs and strong ale. Feckless, in as much as they spent their money as it came — but then they rarely gambled in canal shares! — and brutal, but no more than any honest Englishman who believes in a square fight and winner take all. Resident in huts thrown up as purely temporary accommodation — not always of wood for the Irish who came to join in the bonanza naturally preferred their native turf 'igloos' — reports speak of the "indescribable squalor" in which they lived and yet were unanimous in talking of the smart "uniforms" of the navvies. The names they were known by were usually 'given' rather than the family names of their parents:

ESCAPED FROM JUSTICE

THOMAS BELLYMORE, supposed to be a native of some part of Staffordshire, who stands charged before the Coroner and a Jury of this city, with having lately killed and slayed one GEORGE ROCKETT. He is about five feet six inches high, has dark brown hair, wore a white smock frock and trowsers, and has been lately employed as a labourer upon the Hereford and Gloucester Canal.

The Public are desired to apprehend the said THOMAS BELLYMORE, so that he be secured within some or one of his Majesty's Prisons in this kingdom, to be dealt with according to Law.

Gloucester, Oct. 3 1793   S. COLBORNE, Coroner.

One fears for his fate, navvy or not, if he was to be "within some . . . Prisons"!

En masse there is no doubt that they could be intimidating as James Watt found on the Monkland canal, *"The work done is slovenly, our workmen are bad . . . in short I find myself out of my sphere when I have anything to do with mankind"*, though he had financial troubles, having at one time to raise money from the Thistle Bank on his personal bill (a form of cheque) to pay the wages of his workmen. On the Caledonian canal, *"The workmen are mostly steady industrious men, who work by the piece, and with a good will, because they are regularly paid"* said one commentator, howbeit he was contradicted by another perhaps more critical who caught the navvies at the wrong moment *". . . observing how carelessly the labourers were dabbling with their picks and spades, and how apt they were to look around them at everything which is to be seen, while others were winding slowly out with each a little gravel in a wheelbarrow. . . ."* continuing, that, as the canal works extended for another fifty miles, *". . . my head grew somewhat dizzy, and I felt the same sort of quandary as I used to do formerly when thinking of eternity"*.

The root cause, dissatisfaction with pay, was not necessarily the rate of pay, but simply that they had not been paid at the proper time. Consulting engineers were either paid a flat fee, or fee plus retainer; site engineers a flat salary; contractors by the yard, the agreed length of work being paid not as a lump at the end, but as work progressed, some percentage (5 or 10) being retained as surety for the quality of their work — more or less as a guarantee. Here, too, there were differences; Telford was capable of telling shareholders that inflation meant his contractors had to have more money, whereas the weaker, less influential engineers could do nothing except, one feels, stall for time. This attitude often meant bankruptcy for the contractor who would then give his men an hour's notice and decamp. James Hollinsworth, asked by John Rennie to survey the Salisbury & Southampton canal and explain what was going wrong wrote,

Standedge Tunnel, Huddersfield Narrow Canal

quaintly, *"I should have examined the different Charges on the Spot . . . but this was impossible, the Contractors being confined to their Houses to avoid the Sheriff's Officers who were in search of them. . . .".* It was on this canal that a special call was made for the shareholders to pay a little extra as *"the men have now nearly a month's wages due".* When unpaid the navvies naturally went on the rampage. They might be placated if the company, disbursing a few pounds, agreed to continue the works utilising direct labour. Otherwise the gentry, perforce, would make a collection, pay the men some nominal figure and hope they would go away and not be a drain on parish funds.

Medical care for these men and their families (for most gathered women *"of a certain class and their brats"*) was at best cursory, the local apothecary being paid a nominal fee *"to attend to the wounds"* although the contractors under Telford were instructed to levy a sum (usually a penny per man per week) as an insurance to ensure proper care. There are even records of a bed being subscribed to in the local hospital.

Cholera, a malignant disease almost forgotten by native born UK citizens, was the navvies scourge, it being a matter of some concern to a vicar who noted in 1832, *"I find the cholera has broken out most violently in Paulton [Somerset Coal Canal] and nine died of the disorder the day before yesterday"* and, almost simultaneously, writing about an epidemic spreading through the Black Country, it was claimed that cholera had been conveyed *"in the opinion of the medical men of the town, direct from Bilston [Birmingham Canal Navigations] by the water of the canal"*.

Births, weddings, deaths, seem to have passed mostly without notice; a bitter epitaph by an ex-navvy sums up all:

I'll drink and drink whene'er I can, the drouth is sure to come —
And I will love till lusty life runs out its mortal span,
The end of which is in the ditch for many a navvy man.
The bold navvy man,
The old navvy man,
Safe in a ditch with heels cocked up, so dies the navvy man.

3

THE AGE OF CONSOLIDATION

Initial problems resolved, we find the Directors of a normal waterway standing proudly in the sunshine. One of them carefully takes up a silver shovel, lifts a sod of turf (previously loosened!), places it in 'a fine polished' wheelbarrow, which is then wheeled away by a grinning navvy, suitably dressed in moleskin trousers, canvas shirt, velveteen coat, white felt hat — and hobnailed boots. "Let work commence" comes the order, after the "cutting of the first sod".

In Scotland the 'laying the first stone' ceremony was rather more animated, as we can see from this report of 1769 relating to the Forth & Clyde canal: *"On Wednesday afternoon was laid, by Sir James Dunbar, Bt., one of the committee the first stone of the first Land-lock of the Forth & Clyde navigation, at Dalgrain, near Carron, upon a strong platform of timber and piles that had been prepared as a foundation to this structure. . . . The gentleman attending on this occasion expressed great satisfaction, on being shown the passing of lighters through the temporary lock lately erected as a communication from the canal with the river Carron, for the purpose of carrying stone and other materials for building several of the great locks. This temporary lock being considered as a large working model of the great locks, gave particular entertainment, as being the first lock built in Scotland".*

With luck they will have a good engineer, hardworking contractors, steady navvies and meet with no insurmountable financial difficulties, and a few years later traffic will begin to move, if not along the whole route at least within the stretches open.

Income assured, share prices will rise, even selling at a premium, and in the fullness of time the entire route will be opened. Some three or four weeks after this, the land having consolidated, wharves, warehouses built, lock-keepers appointed, the great opening ceremony could take place. Fattened oxen and beer for the navvies and a cruise plus beanfeast for the proprietors and their friends.

"On Friday, the 18th of June, 1819 — the anniversary of Waterloo — the Lancaster & Kendall Canal was opened by a grand aquatic procession. The Mayor and Corporation, having proceeded to the Canal Basin, preceded by music and flags, entered a fine barge equipped for the occasion, which, with some smaller boats, sailed down the canal, to meet a numerous party of gentlemen from Lancaster. . . . There were in all sixteen boats, ornamented with flags of various devices, and containing three excellent bands of music. Along the whole line every eminence was crowded with spectators, who were highly delighted with the novelty and splendour of the scene. As the procession approached the town it was greeted by the firing of cannon

39

City of Westminster.

GROSVENOR CANAL.

INSTRUCTIONS FOR LOCKMEN.

1.—The Lockmen are under the orders of the Lockmaster.

2.—The Foreman will be in charge during the absence of the Lockmaster.

3.—Any person calling at the Lock on business is to be referred to the Lockmaster, or, in his absence, to the Foreman.

4.—No Lockman will be allowed to leave the Lock during the day, or when on duty at night, without the permission of the Lockmaster.

5.—The Foreman is responsible for the cleanliness of the Lock and its surroundings.

6.—The Lockman on night duty must attend at once to all calls made by Lightermen, and call the Lockmaster when necessary.

7.—Every barge is to be passed into the Canal on its arrival, unless instructions to the contrary are given by the Lockmaster.

8.—No barge is to be allowed to pass through the Lock (in or out) without a Lighterman on board.

9.—Every barge approaching the Canal, which has never before passed through the Lock, is to be measured by means of a rod provided for that purpose, before it is allowed to enter the Lock.

10.—No barge of a greater width than 18 ft. 6 in. is to be allowed to enter the Lock.

11.—Barges or other craft will only be passed in and out of the Canal at 1½ hours before and after high water, except under special circumstances, when permission must be obtained from the Lockmaster.

JOHN HUNT,
Town Clerk.

City Hall,
   Charing Cross Road,
      April, 1907.

Instructions for Lockmen

"Water for the supply of the Newport Pagnell Canal may be taken from the Grand Junction Canal"

placed on Castle Hill, on one side of the valley, and in Chapel Close on the other. . . . The packets, &c., arrived in the Basin about four o'clock when the company disembarked and went in procession through the streets to the Town Hall, where a sumptuous dinner was provided. . . . A ball at the King's Arms, in the evening, concluded the festivities of the occasion".

Somewhere in this drab 20th century we seem to have lost the 'sense of occasion'; contrast the brief dry notice as each stretch of motorway is opened with the bonfires that were lit on every hillock between the Trent and the Mersey when the Grand Trunk canal was opened in 1777. Imagine the fervour with which the bells were rung at every church between Birmingham and Wolverhampton on the 14th September 1772 when the Birmingham canal was opened. Imagine the wagons laden with full hogsheads of ale that groaned their way to Chesterfield when that navigation first passed boats through. Why the very wenches of the villages put on their finery to greet the boats on the Leeds & Liverpool canal when *"At nine the proprietors sailed up the canal in their barge preceded by another, filled with music, with colours flying, &c. and returned about one. They were saluted with two royal salutes of twenty-one guns each . . . and welcomed with repeated shouts of the numerous crowd assembled on the bank who made a most cheerful and agreeable sight. The gentlemen then adjourned to a tent on the quay where a cold collation was set out for themselves and their friends. From thence they went in procession to George's Coffee House where an elegant dinner was provided. The workmen, 215 in number, walked first with their tools on their shoulders and cockades in their hats, and were afterwards plentifully regaled at a dinner pro-*

"Pleasure Boats may be used toll free" — even in 1860

vided for them. The bells rung all day and the greatest joy and order prevailed on the occasion". and a holiday with pay was declared so that no one should miss the fun.

With the navigation open, unless the proprietors were enthusiastic campaigners, they consolidated their gains, for a while at least. Warehouses had to be extended, more stables built, boat services including 'Packets' for passengers needed to be arranged.

In 1824 the Edinburgh & Glasgow Union Canal *"Owing to the rapid increase of trade . . . the present basin at Port Hopetoun has been found inadequate to accommodate the numerous barges which are now plying on that navigation. The Canal Company have therefore resolved to construct another basin, in addition to the present one, considerably larger than it, and in the same neighbourhood. . . . Within the last few months the coal-trade has been carried on to an immense extent, and is still to be greatly augmented. All sorts of building-materials, for which there is at present in Edinburgh an uncommon demand, are now brought by this conveyance. . . . A great impulse seems to have been given lately in building, both dwelling houses and warehouses, in the vicinity of the Canal basin. A fine large building, for the luggage-boat companies are now getting up at the basin, upon the projecting square used as a landing-place for passengers; and several offices for the coal-companies have just been completed. . . . Several boats from this quarry are constantly employed — each carrying between 40 and 50 tons, and making generally three trips in a day. Such are the expectations of a still increasing trade on this Canal, that one boat-builder, in the vicinity of the basin, has contracted, since the middle of summer, for building ten boats".* In true Scottish fashion, wasting nothing, one other new traffic had come into being *"It is not a little extraordinary to find that the cow-feeders of Edinburgh are now supplied with draff from a distillery at the distance of 35 miles. One brings about 40 tons weekly of this article".*

Minor extentions to collieries, quarries and the like needed careful consideration, preference being given to horse-drawn tramroads rather than an arm off

42

the canal; the former brought income without worry, the latter needed water which in all probability was already in short supply, a bugbear even the best canals could never quite overcome. Still, new sources could be sought — artesian wells dug, steam pumps installed to back-pump water within lock flights and even, on the Wey & Arun and the Thames & Severn canals, windmills pumping from spring fed wells, although far cheaper than steam-pumps which consumed about one ton of coal each twenty-four hours and needed 'tenters', these windmills were somewhat unreliable.

The odd upset personage, often a vicar in his parsonage, had to be placated, as on the Manchester, Bolton & Bury canal when it was directed that the packet steerer must cease *"to blow his horn when passing the church near Windsor Bridge on Sunday evening as it annoys the congregation";* in Scotland the Moderator of the Free Presbytery Church at Abertarff requested that a stop be put to all *"unnecessary labour"* on Sundays and Mr. Haddon *"a great manufacturer, employing 3000 persons"* complained that the Inveraray Canal drew water off the Don to the *"hurt of his mills".* But these were humdrum matters to be dealt with by the Secretary.

But what now? A rival canal is promoted? How dare they! In no way would they tolerate this! Having grown used to their dividends the existing shareholders had no intention whatsoever of letting the smallest particle drop from their table and would seek to hinder the newcomer in any way possible. However, they had a good precedent, for when in 1764 a Mr. Roe suggested building a canal between Liverpool and Macclesfield it was passed by the House of Commons but rejected by the Lords *". . . by the influence of the Duke of Bridgewater, whose navigation had been opened for the conveyance of goods but a short time before".*

Somerset Coal Canal, Radstock, 1967

Her Majesty Queen Victoria — Bridgewater Canal, October 1851

Even if it appeared that the plans for the upstart navigation might pass through Parliament then still the opposition would fight on, mainly over the question of water supply. It being reasonable to protect the older company's supply, a clause in the newcomer's Act would stipulate that a stop or regulating lock was to be inserted between the two navigations and the weir-levels on the new waterway arranged in such a manner, by being higher, that they always paid a 'water-fee' to the older company for every passing boat, thus *"Water for the supply of this canal* (Newport Pagnell) *may be taken from the Grand Junction Canal, under certain restrictions, the Newport Company making a lock at the union of the canals, with its upper gates one foot above the top water level of the Grand Junction, such lock to be maintained at the cost of the Newport Company"*. High toll rates for through traffic would ensure that no financial loss would accrue, and reasonably enough both the toll clerks and lock-keepers at the regulating lock, although employees of the existing company, would have their wages paid by the new company.

Sometimes a wealthy company would find they had an excess of money. On the Glamorganshire, where it was set at 8%, and other canals (varying between 5% and 15%) the maximum dividend paid to shareholders was limited by their respective Acts of Parliament. The Somerset Coal Canal had, perforce, to accept many restrictions, it being stipulated that *"The profits of this concern are not to exceed 10 per cent, but after £1,000 is accumulated and placed in government securities, as a fund for contingencies, the tolls on coals are to be lowered. Husbandry and pleasure boats 12 feet long and 5 feet wide may be used toll free ..."* When not disallowed a toll-fee

Water turnpike with unequivocal instructions

period might be declared — especially where the shareholders operated boats — or extra fees paid to use up the cash, the directors having carried out duties 'beyond the call'. But if there was still too much cash in the exchequer another outlet, that financially should be self-regenerating, was to invest in a waterway to be newly built and one that, with luck, would bring traffics onto 'our' waterway.

During the building of the Wilts & Berks canal (a rather poorly agricultural canal) the Somerset Coal canal had invested money in the hope that it would open up new markets for their staple diet — coal. Alas in 1824 we find that the Secretary of the Wilts & Berks had to write (as he had before and did subsequently) to coal merchants: *"Annexed I send you a Copy of the Coal Canal Co's resolution as to a further Drawback [discount] of 1s [5p] per ton on Coal carried to Wallingford and Benson via the Wilts and Berks canal. You will please inform me what your present selling price is and pledge yourself to reduce the shilling to your customers otherwise the additional Drawback will not be continued"*. The Somerset Coal canal Secretary had found to his horror that coal brought down the Oxford canal was being sold rather than best Somersetshire fuel!

The Somerset Coal canal was in many ways one of the 'Ruritanian' concerns that provide much astonishment today, for when it was realised that a height difference of some 46′ (14 m) had to be surmounted, a mechanical boat-lift patented by a Mr. Robert Weldon (No. 1892 of June 19th, 1792) was proposed in lieu of locks. Regrettably this failed, brilliant in its conception, neither the materials

New warehouses — Huddersfield Narrow Canal

nor the workmanship were equal to the task although according to one writer who claims to have seen it in operation *"It will ever remain a memorable proof of the superior mechanical abilities of its very ingenious inventor"*. However, they did persevere as long as possible, advertising in 1799: *"The Committee of the Somerset Coal Canal being desirous of having the present CAISSON CISTERN at Combhay, near Bath, RE-BUILT, and made Water-tight, (and it being probable that other Cisterns of a similar or greater depth may be built on the Line of Canal) invite all Masons, competent to such an undertaking, to deliver proposals for effecting and compleating such Work, (sealed) to Mr. Weldon at Combhay, on or before the 3rd day of June next . . . and Contractors will be required to enter into proper security for the Cistern holding water"*. This last was the crux of the matter, water having leaked between the stones of the 'cistern' walls, and by causing them to bulge, jammed the whole works. The leakage, we are told, was due to *"the masons being either too ignorant or too remiss in their part of the work"*.

The project was shortly afterwards abandoned and instead, in 1800, an inclined plane was built as a temporary expedient while the company scratched around to raise the necessary £45,000 in order to build the Combe Hay flight of locks, the relics of which may still be seen striding round the hill. This inclined plane — a 'whimsey' or 'Jenny' road in the engineers' parlance — must have been a tedious thing to operate for its use meant that coal (and other goods) had to travel in boxes, these boxes being either loaded into boats at the colliery or the coal transhipped from boat to box, lowered and again transhipped. Either way breakages were high and the whole operation — for each box held only two tons

46

— incredibly slow and expensive. Faced with building a further flight of locks on their Radstock branch they, wisely, built a tramroad instead.

With the Turnpikes still offering some rivalry in the carriage of goods, it was normally only a matter of weeks after the opening of a waterway that they, in turn, took passengers from the stage coaches. On a lock-free canal — the Bridgewater canal or a long summit pound, say, the 14 miles of the Worcester & Birmingham canal from Birmingham to Kings Norton — a steady 4mph could be maintained without stress; where locks were involved the handling of these was reduced to a fine art. As passenger boats ran to a strict timetable and had precedence over all other boats, it was not difficult for the lock-keeper to have the locks ready. On the Manchester, Bolton & Bury canal the postillion was ordered to sound his horn in advance — but not on Sundays — and the boat could clear six locks in under ten minutes, but when Queen Victoria passed along the Crinan canal in 1847 on her outward journey she recorded in her diary that *". . . the eleven locks we had to go through were tedious, and instead of the passage lasting one hour and a half it lasted upwards of two and a half"*. However, homeward bound, the company having had the imagination to station a piper at each lock, she was happier despite the fact that it rained throughout the journey.

On northern waterways, taking advantage of the wider channel, great comfort was offered. The boat *". . . was, in fact, a floating house, with seven windows on each side; and affording to those passengers who preferred an airy seat, a flat roof for the purpose, as well as comfortable benches thereon, firmly screwed down, to sit upon; those who occupied the cabin enjoyed the usual accommodation of a steam-boat. Though built purposely for speed and light draft, this vessel was firm, and steady in the water; she was indeed two boats linked together, with a double keel, and open channel between both; — a moveable cast-iron cutwater fixed a-head, when lifted up was completely out of the way, but when down formed a very acute angle, and brought as it were the two boats into one, it prevented the stream from filling the hollow channel, and obstructing the progress"*.

In many ways, life 150 years ago must have been more enjoyable. We, who are now so blase, would pass the 696 yards (636 m) of Falkirk tunnel on the Edinburgh & Glasgow Union canal without batting an eyelid. Not so in 1823 — *"When the passengers see the wide chasm, and the distant light glimmering through the lonely dark arch of nearly half a mile in length, they are struck with feelings of awe; and as they proceed through it, and see the damp roof above their heads, feel the chill rarified air, and hear every sound re-echoing through the gloomy cavern, their feelings are wound to the highest pitch"*.

In Wales, on the Tennant canal, the thrifty operators of a packet boat between Neath and Port Tennant, in addition to passengers carried *"parcels, shop goods, corn, flour and light merchandize"*. Elsewhere barrels of beer, eggs, chicken and geese were among fellow travellers.

As the stagecoaches whittled their times down, so the canal companies — especially those in Scotland — applied a little science to the design of their boats with the result that *"If any one had stated five years ago, that by improvements in the build of Canal Passage Boats, a speed of ten miles per hour would be regularly maintained on Canal routes; and that the charges to passengers carried at this speed, would be the same as at the previous slow speed of four or five miles per hour; that in one small district of Scotland alone, distances amounting in all to nine hundred miles each day . . . should be performed by these improved Light Boats at the above speed . . . the assertation would have been received with unlimited ridicule. . . . Yet such is now the case".*

Towards the end of their final flowering this canal, the Glasgow, Paisley & Ardrossan was able to maintain twelve boats per day each way between Paisley & Glasgow with an average payload of just over 100 souls per trip.

To the shareholders and directors of a successful waterway the sight of raw materials and finished products alike moving on 'their' water, the hubbub of passengers waiting for the Packet, the new warehouses, and the apparently insatiable demands of shippers and traders for more boats and more facilities must have seemed like a dream come true; but dry rot, or at least iron-mould, was working to bring the whole so-secure edifice tumbling down.

4

THE TRAMROAD AGE

When a canal and a rail enthusiast meet, the one matter they can both agree on is that canals gave dual impetus to the building of railways both by their experiments with tramroads and — sadly — by their greed.

There are technical differences between tramroads and railways — although the words were interchangeable over two hundred years ago — but for our purposes we may take tramroads as being, basically, horsedrawn feeders to canals, while the railways began with the Liverpool & Manchester railway in 1826. Some canal folk also claim that railways ended their golden age when, by their own greed, they led to the building of the Manchester Ship Canal!

The primary reasons why tramroads became so popular with canal managements were two-fold. Firstly the lines of the bulk of long distance, or awkwardly situated, canals involved either tunnelling or long flights of locks, both causing much expense and delay and leading to a distinct lack of income — at a time when vast interest payments were being made on borrowed money. The second, and more obvious if less vital, reason (because it was appreciated) was that tramroads could go where canals, by reason of their dependence on water supplies, would find the terrain impassable. There was, and is, no physical reason why a canal should not be built up and down Ben Nevis but the summit, or top level, pound would be so short that the first boat up, by drawing water from above in order to ascend, would probably leave insufficient for it to move, let alone go down!

One can, for an example of this problem, consider the Huddersfield Narrow canal, where 42 locks took it up to 436′ (133 m) to the summit which was, more or less, the length of Standedge tunnel — 5451 yds (4984 m) — and it then immediately descended 334.5′ (102 m) by way of a further 33 locks. Described as a losing speculation, only one boat could pass through the tunnel at a time as they were 'legged' through by men lying on the boat and pushing with their feet against the tunnel walls, taking about two hours for the passage. Despite reservoirs, in summer the payload dropped from the official 24 tons to 10! A tramroad would have served as well or even better. Similarly the Lancaster Canal Company faced with the stiff climb over Walton Summit between Preston and Walton built 'as a temporary expedient' a tramroad between the two ends of the waterway. Temporary or not it was opened in 1805 and remained in situ until 1857!

Grand Junction Canal after completion, 1819

Another bisected canal was the Grand Junction at Blisworth. Here the first attempt to cut the tunnel was flooded out and abandoned in March 1797. When the waterway was reaching towards Stoke Bruerne in 1799 it was all too apparent that the toll-road — "a miserable rutted track" — was useless as a means of carrying much tonnage. William Jessop, the consulting engineer, suggested a tramroad would be more suitable despite the fact it had to climb 192′ from Stoke Bruerne and descend 136′ to Blisworth over a distance of 3½ miles. The contract was let to Benjamin Outram, the foremost exponent of tramroads, for the "Blisworth Hill Railway", at a total cost of £9,750 including four cranes and 80 waggons. The navvies, who presumably preferred canals to tramroads, gave some trouble and the local Magistrates were forced to sort out the *"Disputes between Masters and Labourers"* and had to enforce *"the more decent Observances of the Sabbath"* but notwithstanding this the line was opened by the end of 1800 and ran, with all the concomitant difficulties of double transhipment, until 1805, when the tunnel was opened. The tramplates are believed to have been reutilised on the tramway which connected Gayton Wharf with Northampton prior to the completion of that lock flight in 1815.

When tramroads were to be regarded as an extention of a waterway, the proposal might be built-in when first applying for authorisation, although this was probably a decision made after some acrimonious debate between protagonists of a through stillwater navigation and of a hybrid canal/tramroad line.

The Ashby-de-la-Zouch canal was planned to be an all-water line with branches to Ticknall and Cloudhill although it was anticipated that 252′ (78 m) of lockage would be required for these branches and, perhaps warily, the proprietors made available two quotations, one for the whole of the works at £138,238 and the other for building only the 'main line' at £27,316 11.4½d. Engineered by Robert Whitworth the preferred latter was opened in May 1805. A total of 14 miles of tramroad were eventually brought into use.

By contrast the Peak Forest Tramway was designated as one of the "Railways or Stone Roads" to be built under the PFC's Act of 1794. Although this waterway was to have terminated at Chapel Milton, the engineer, Benjamin Outram, decided in view of the over-riding gradient that a tramroad would suit the proprietors' purposes better from Bugsworth to Loads Knowle. The basic function of both canal and tramroad was the carriage of lime for "the enrichment of the soil" and of limestone necessary for the repair of the rival turnpike! Rather improbably the tramroad remained in use, although railway owned, until 1926.

The Cromford & High Peak Railway was described as the "skyscraping railway with its corkscrew curves that seem to have been laid out by a mad Archimedes endeavouring to square the circle" and was a replacement for an earlier, slightly lunatic, plan to build a canal from Cromford basin which would have had to ascend 710′ (216 m) to Ladmanlow and then descend 747′ (228 m) back to the junction with the Peak Forest canal at Whaley Bridge. As the average lock imparts a lift of 9′-10′ (3 m) and this route was only 33 miles long, the idea daunted even that redoubtable engineer Josias Jessop who suggested, and recommended, the tramroad, emphasising the financial savings involved in a tramroad

Transhipment, Derby Canal Tramroad c.1900

rather than a navigation and quoting a total cost of £149,206 in lieu of Rennie's canal estimate of £650,000. Jessop stated *"The comparatively small expense of forming Railways will be a cause of extending our resources and finding new channels for capital and industry, that would forever have been neglected, if there were only the more expensive modes of Roads or Canals to resort to; the first being expensive in the carriage, the latter in the execution"*. Opened throughout on 6th July 1831 it was a financial loss to the shareholders although *"advantageous to the populace . . . for the inhabitants have for long felt the inconvenience and expense of bringing coal from a distance . . . where the quantity taken by a horse must necessarily be small"*. Two years after the opening the first steam loco was delivered, superceding horse-power, but it was not until 1862 that the whole was leased to the L & NWR.

Long before the Cromford & High Peak Railway was a twinkle in its engineers eye the 8¼ miles of the Mansfield and Pinxton railway was already functioning, giving the inhabitants of the former town access to Birmingham and London via the Pinxton Branch of the Cromford canal. Opened 13th April, 1819, the proprietors quite cheerfully took the first waggonload of coal to arrive in Mansfield, piled it up in the market-place and, setting it alight by way of a celebration, burnt the whole lot!

Unusually using oxen rather than horses this successful tramroad was sold to a railway company in 1847.

One thousand miles of tramroads connected to canals are known to have been built, opening previously inaccessible areas, fed to and by a canal. Having served this purpose they died but were, in effect, cuckoos in the canal nest.

One particularly odious bird was the Surrey Iron Railway, which was built by virtue of an Act of Parliament dated 21st May 1801, some four weeks before the Croydon canal was authorised. Both forms of transport ran from the Thames (the canal via the Grand Surrey), both served the same town — one with a mere 7,000 inhabitants — both supplied *"Croydon and its vicinity with coal, deals, and general merchandize"* and as back-carriage moved *"agricultural produce, chalk, fire-stone, fuller's earth, &c. to London"*. The tramroad cost about £60,000, the canal double that figure, and indulging in ruinous competition neither paid their shareholders more than a 1% dividend. In 1836 the canal shareholders were glad enough to accept £40,000 from the London & Croydon railway for their waterway, such parts of the canal that were required for the 'new steam road' being de-watered in 1836 — although the 'triumph' of the Surrey Iron Railway was short lived as it was itself abandoned eight years later.

One tramroad engineer, almost forgotten in the rail stampede of Brunels, Stephensons, Lockes and their ilk, was George Overton, who, nevertheless, should always be remembered for he built the Penydarren Tramroad, describing it thus:

". . . I completed a tramroad from the bottom of an inclined plane near Dowlais Works to the navigation house on the Glamorganshire Canal [Abercynon] a distance of upwards of nine miles, the fall on some parts of the road being upwards of one inch per yard, and on the remain-

Successor to the Surrey Iron Railway. Steam tranroad in use during building of Canada Dock, c.1900

ing portion varying from two to six inches per chain. Upon this road . . . a single horse continued for some time to haul ten tons, and bring back the empty trams, travelling regularly a distance of nineteen miles per day"

On this tramroad on 14th February 1804 — as the result of a £1,000 wager between two ironmasters, (Samuel Homfray who said it would, and Richard Crawshay who pooh-poohed the whole idea) — a steam engine, designed by Francis Trevithick, was persuaded to drag ten tons of iron and seventy men for the whole distance; the first authenticated instance of steam railway passenger haulage. Such was the speed of advancement in transport within the British Isles that only 17 years before (1787) William Jessop had recommended that, *"It may . . . be found advisable instead of a Rail Way to make a Stone Road, which will be done at less than half the expence of the other; for I am inclined to think that such a Road, properly formed, covered with small beaten Stone, and used only by Carriages with Cylindrical Wheels, may answer every purpose of a Railway"*.

And, still progressing at breakneck speed, only 22 years later the proprietors of the Liverpool and Manchester Railway were given permission to "make and maintain a Railway or Tramroad" between those two towns. By its nature it represented the make-or-break point in canal and railway history. Hitherto although tramroads were busy enough they were (with odd minor exceptions like the Surrey Iron Railway) subjugated to waterways. Had this enterprise failed then canals would have remained, for a while at least, the premier means of transport; its success turned the whole transport world on its head.

In 1790 the available navigation links between these two cities could, just, cope with the demands of both the populations and manufactories. But, regard by 1821 the population of Liverpool, brought about by the voracious needs of factories, had increased by a staggering 114% from 55,732 in 1790 to 118,972; while Manchester and Salford more than doubled — 57,000 to 134,000. Despite minor physical improvements, congestion on the waterways had led to a lowering of transport standards; as the population increased this could only get worse. The

53

cotton trade until the late 1780s relied on supplies from the West Indies brought to London but while only 503 bags of American cotton arrived in the UK in 1792, by 1823 over 412,000 bags were handled in Liverpool, out of a total quantity of 573,000 brought into the country! The primary reason for the increase was simply that from 1787 onward steam powered mills replaced the traditional waterwheel. Unlike a waterwheel a steam engine could work as long as required, winter and summer alike — in fact longer than its human attendants could cope with — increased power meant increased output of finished goods (which needed shifting) and increased input of raw materials which had to be available day in, day out. These early steam engines also had voracious appetites for coal; that also must be on site when required.

The basic channels available for commerce between Liverpool and Manchester included the Turnpike which was in surprisingly bad condition, although by 1825 coach services offered around 800 passenger seats per day, taking three hours. Pack-horses taking ten hours and wagons two days or so, offered good services.

Road was overshadowed by water routes one of which, the Mersey & Irwell, after some short cuts had been made between 1800 and 1825, offered 57 flats (a type of barge) of around 30 ton capacity each of which could cover, in theory at least, the 42 miles of estuary and river in twelve hours, charging, in 1826, 75p tolls and carriage per ton of cotton, 54p for coal and 50p for flour. The Leeds & Liverpool canal via Wigan and Leigh offered some possibilities but was cruelly handicapped by a higher mileage and a toll rate of 46p; the carriers charge would make this double before the goods arrived. The time involved — some 3 days — hardly improved matters and the supplementary flyboat service which reduced this to a mere (theoretical) 24 hours cost an additional £1 per ton. The third, most important, intransigent, and vociferous waterway was the Bridgewater. Following the death of the Duke of Bridgewater in 1803, his vast network of mines, canal interests and land was administered by three trustees, two of whom from their own choice became sequacious to Robert Haldane Bradshaw, the Duke's Agent. As long as profits were made (some £120,000 per annum on average) the Marquess of Stafford, nephew and heir to the Duke's fortune, saw no reason to interfere with whatever Bradshaw did; it is doubtful even whether he could, for the terms of the Duke's will gave Bradshaw extraordinary powers.

Apart from carefully extracting the maximum dues from shippers he bought up, on behalf of the 'Duke's interest' any land that might possibly serve as a site for warehousing. By eliminating any rivalry there he also made it virtually impossible for any independent carrier to be too competitive. Finally tolls were so arranged that the Mersey & Irwell and Bridgewater navigations were in no sense rivals thus — the Leeds & Liverpool canal hardly being competitive, and anyway relying on the Bridgewater canal for access to Manchester — attaining a virtual monopoly. While the loyalty of Bradshaw to his master was of a kind

we can barely comprehend, nevertheless by 1822 the shippers and factory owners felt enough was enough and called upon William James — a leading railway
exponent — to carry out a survey of possible routes. Not unsurprisingly history
repeated itself, as colliers, hired by landowners who were also shareholders in
one or both navigations, set upon the survey teams much as the Duke's men had
been treated some 64 years previously. Although for various reasons the plan for
the railway was then held in abeyance, Bradshaw sensing trouble announced
that from 8th December 1823 tolls would be reduced by 25%, extraneous charges
abolished, and warehouse rates cut. Generous indeed but too late. Joseph San-
dars, Secretary to the Provisional Committee of the Liverpool & Manchester put
forward an unanswerable argument:

*"A Rail-road will enable passengers to travel between Liverpool and Manchester at the rate
of 10 or 12 miles an hour, at one-half the price they pay now. A Rail-road will prevent any
future combination to raise freights, and it would make the Trustees of his Grace of Bridgewater as anxious to let and sell warehouses and land, as they have been to grasp and retain
them".*

Indeed he went further by quoting to the canal companies the falacious argu-
ments that had been used against them.

"About the year 1765, when Canals were projected, numerous pamphlets
were published to show their danger and impolicy. The Turnpike Trustees and
the owners of Pack Horses saw danger to their interest, and they made the
landed proprietors believe that Canals would supersede the use of horses, and
thereby diminish the consumption of hay and oats. The parties joined, and by
their representation that internal navigation would destroy the coasting trade,
and consequently the nursery for seamen, succeeded for a year or two in preven-
ting several important undertakings which were contemplated, and amongst the
rest, the Trent & Mersey Navigation. What has been the effect of Canals? They
have increased trade, commerce, and manufactures — they have increased turnpike roads — they have increased the number of horses and the growth of hay
and corn — they have increased both the coasting trade and the number of seamen. Canals have done well for the country, just as high roads and pack horses
had done before Canals were established. . . ."

Relaxing on the Brecon & Abergavenny Canal, c.1890

Of the battles and skirmishes that then raged, including one over a proposed Act that was won by the canal interests in 1825, is a story that must be told by a railway historian — enough that on 5th May 1826 the L & MR was given the green light to proceed about its business.

Although the Liverpool & Manchester was not to be opened until 1830, nevertheless their Public Relations department worked overtime to gain the approval of 'the people who count' and on 14th November 1829 we have an eye-witness report on exactly what railway travel was like in the earliest days.

"*. . . Today we have had a lark of a very high order. Lady Wilton sent over yesterday from Knowsley to say that the loco motive machine was to be upon the railway at such a place at 12 o'clock for the Knowsley party to ride in if they liked, and inviting this house to be of the party. So of course we were at our post in 3 carriages and some horsemen at the hour appointed. I had the satisfaction, for I can't call it pleasure, of taking a trip of five miles in it, which we did in just a quarter of an hour — that is, 20 miles an hour. As accuracy upon this subject was my great object, I held my watch in my hand at starting, and all the time; and as it had a second hand, I knew I could not be deceived; and so it turned out there was not the difference of a second between the coachee or conductor and myself. But observe, during these five miles, the machine was occasionally made to put itself out or go it; and then we went at the rate of 23 miles an hour, and just with the same ease as to motion or absence of friction as the other reduced pace. But the quickest motion is to me frightful; it is really flying, and it is impossible to divest yourself of the notion of instant death to all upon the least accident happening. It gave me a headache which has not left me yet. . . . The smoke is very inconsiderable indeed, but sparks of fire are abroad in some quantity; one burnt Miss de Ros's cheek, another a hole in Lady Maria's silk pelisse, and a third a hole in some one else's gown. Altogether I am extremely glad indeed to have seen this miracle, and to have travelled in it. Had I thought worse of it than I do, I should have had the curiosity to try it; but, having done so, I am quite satisfied with my first achievement being my last*".

Not everyone seemed to fall for the blandishments of the railway, even five years after this, opposition was often expressed — if fancifully. "*Goodman, or any of the good whips, will take you from the Golden Cross [London] at a steady trot, in four hours and a half, to Brighton. Now nobody — except, indeed, courtiers and expectants — can have any business at Brighton; it is a place for health and relaxation — travelling itself is relaxation to a Cockney — and as for health, whether a man bathe, or be shampooed at four o'clock or six, can make no great difference. What upon earth, then, can be the use of a railroad to Brighton?*"

5
MIDDLE AGE

As can happen to people, not all waterways had a true middle-age. Some, due to arrested physical development, passed — like the Kington, Leominster & Stourport canal — straight from puny youth to enfeebled senility; others, precocious or stalwart enough, appeared to be immutable, their very 'being' and trade as sure as the rise of the sun. In truth though, the prosperous middle age of Britain's navigations was short enough, at best 60 years, and even at their peak they had to contend for the cream of traffics with the turnpike. It is curious to reflect on how these twain, both vanquished by the infamous 'tea-kettle on wheels' have subsequently re-established themselves; the one is now our only Government-approved transport method, the other a hedonists' paradise.

The first waterway to be truly prosperous was undoubtedly the Duke of Bridgewater's, and it is pleasant to think of him sitting back in 1761 undoing the bottom waistcoat button, dabbing lips with a napkin, gazing at a glass of cutwater-brought port and heaving a sigh of relief.

But when Harecastle tunnel finally came into use in 1777 after an 11 year battle and with it the Grand Trunk canal, did Wedgwood and his minions sit back and wait for the tills to ring? No, is the simple answer.

Disregard for now the turnpike and regard the other manifold problems. First of all people in the late 18th and early 19th centuries were, even more than us, slow moving and unwilling to change the habits of centuries. "It's all very well and good" one imagines a farmer saying to his neighbour, "but is this new-fangled canal reliable? Old Joe the carter, he takes my corn and brings me back coal and all the other oddments every Wednesday, regular, as his Dad did in my father's time; but how do I know my corn won't be wet? I reckon I'll wait a year or two and see how things go". A year or two later the farmers meet again. "Ow do. I hear the Cut has cut coal prices by nearly a half" says the neighbour. "Ah, but" replies our farmer, "I hears there's a lot of slack among it and when I wrote to the Canal Company they reckoned I'd have to pay for a wharf and then cartage to the farm. Reckon I'll wait another year or two and see how things go". Conjectural? Not so, for we find in canal records that trade was poorer than expected due to the difficulty in inducing *"tradesmen and farmers to adopt a mode of carrying different to that to which they have been accustomed"*, and that in summer *"coal is stocked in excess at the [Town] wharf owing to the unwillingness of local men to take more*

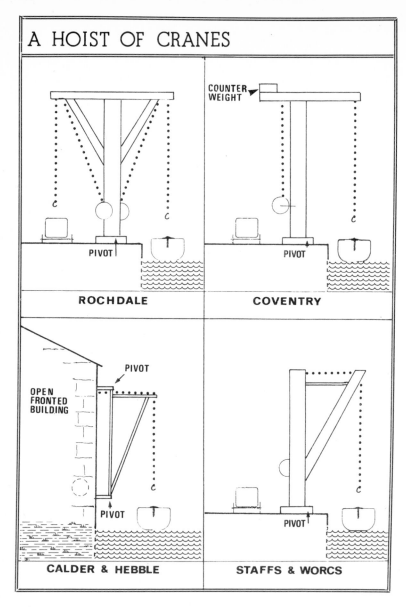

A HOIST OF CRANES

ROCHDALE

COVENTRY

COUNTER WEIGHT

PIVOT

CALDER & HEBBLE

STAFFS & WORCS

OPEN FRONTED BUILDING

PIVOT

A hoist of cranes

than their normal weekly quota" — anticipating their channel might freeze in winter the canal company had hoped that customers would stockpile, instead the scheme backfired.

The basic requirements of an efficiently run canal are that adequate loading staithes (or wharves) be available, preferably offering covered warehousing facilities, that a boat or boats be expected at the time when the goods arrive for onward carriage and that, again, warehousing should be available at destination. Furthermore cranes should be on site — preferably free of charge — and whether or not they are, adequate manpower should be just waiting for work. And above all, this service must be regular.

In exchange for all these facilities the canal company must charge the bare minimum tolls, ensure an adequate supply of water in summer, arrange an ice-free channel in winter, carry out maintenance works at the least inconvenient time to the customer (preferably in the middle of the night!) and arrange that its personnel, whatever the circumstances, should be willing, courteous and 'doff their caps'.

The provision of warehousing was ever a problem for even when the company was wealthy, the purchase of land adjacent to the channel, which not unsurprisingly rose in price when the utility of the canal was realised, was still a matter requiring deep consideration.

To the proprietors these facilities were, anyway, regarded with somewhat jaundiced eyes for often their authorising acts stated just what revenue they might expect. The Lea river might only get 3d (1½p) per ton "For all Goods, Wares and Merchandize remaining on the Wharf Forty-eight Hours", after that they got 6d (2½p) although that was little enough bearing in mind that labour to discharge goods was borne by the Company. On the Sheffield & South Yorkshire Navigation *"Goods taken away before the expiration of Seventy-two Hours, not to pay any Wharfage Rate"* although after that a table was required (and a human calculator) for rates varied according to the nature of the goods.

If it appeared that there was any risk of the Company having a monopoly in facilities then Parliament in its wisdom might, as with the Manchester, Bolton & Bury canal, permit *"Lords of manors, and proprietors of land on the line to build Wharfs, cranes, weigh-beams and warehouses, and if not, then the company may build the same"*. The Company having exercised its option they were allowed 1d per ton, although this was a flat rate where *"coal, iron and limestone"* were concerned, *covering the first three weeks stay!* On the Newport Pagnall canal 'Lords of the Manor', or the Company, having erected wharves, could charge 6d (2½p) per ton but coal and similar goods could remain on the wharves for three months.

The change in the appearance of a town was such that commentators of the period drew their readers' attention to it. *"The town of Wakefield is the emporium of grain for the manufacturing districts, by means of a canal communication to the north, east, the west and the south, all over the country. The western line, towards Manchester, diverges in*

Paddington Canal, 1820

two forks; the one proceeding through the Huddersfield Tunnel, an underground channel of three miles and a quarter in length, and the other by a more circuitous track through Rochdale. Large shipments of corn are brought hither from the counties of Norfolk and Lincolnshire by the Trent and Humber. . . . It is not easy to form an idea of the very enormous extent of the storehouses . . . without the actual use of the eyes; they really seem calculated to hold under their roofs, not only all the corn in England but that of the Baltic into the bargain".

When the line of the canal was mooted, no doubt such matters were taken into consideration, although the heady scent of success may well have led to certain clauses in the enabling Act to be overlooked, otherwise how else could the Coventry canal have agreed to the following: *". . . no Charge to be made for the Use of the Crane, which the Company are required to erect on the Bank of the Canal. . . ."?* The mind boggles — just think of that lost revenue! At least they had the consolation that Parliament did not specify the type of crane to be used. The most sensible was probably the double-arm type to be found on the Rochdale, which was fixed on a wharf or pier-head and so framed and braced that it balanced exactly when turning on a pivot at the bottom. Although counterbalanced, like its single armed cou-

60

sin, three or more men were required to operate it. In most cases two men wound enormous handles geared to the lifting chain and the other operated the retaining ratchet and the brake, this was (and occasionally on the British Waterways Board's maintenance yards, still is) merely a band of asbestos-type substance running on a gigantic fly-wheel. Application on a frosty day can be interesting — the pyrotechnics rivalling a grindstone as gravity grabs the five ton or so load and the poor mortal breakman hangs on for grim life! Movement around the pedestal is again, mandraulic, and the number of men used depends on how viscous the oil on the rollers is! Wood or wrought iron were normal for the main structure — no doubt reasonable when new, one boatman in 1820 had the unhappy experience of both the corn bags he was discharging plus the arm of the crane whistle past his nose and through the boat's bottom. One hopes he had many a free pint for his tale!

The use of water and steam propelled cranes must have added their own risks although reducing the purely physical effort involved, but even a horse-gin has its disadvantage — or was the crane operator allowed the dung for his garden? The records do not say.

The sheer volume of goods moving along a canal can even now give some idea of the reason for many warehouses. The minimum number of narrow boats arriving at a wharf was about 50 per week, each with a cubic capacity of some 1,050 cu.ft. and carrying some 25-30 tons. If one quarter of this required covered accommodation and the goods could be stacked 6' (2 m) high that building would have to measure some 50' x 100' (465 m²) to hold just this one consignment and, if the recipient was so minded he could leave that lot lying about for three months! *"To this day Messrs. Firth retain their special reputation in steel; and they have also a high name for the best brands of foreign iron, of which they are large importers, and in which they deal as merchants. Their wharfs on the Sheffield Canal are a model of order and neatness — the 'stacks' of fine foreign iron being piled up as beautifully as if they were designed to remain there for ever, each stack representing some £20,000 or more in value".*

Naturally the style of wharf varied according to the inclination of the providers and the nature of the anticipated trade. The simplest, most suitable for the occasional churn of milk plus (at different times) manure, was, and is, no more than a row of wooden posts with planking on top. A coal wharf, the next size up, would probably have a facing of stone and stables adequate for one or two horses and their forage. Where it was anticipated that trade would be heavy a mini-village would be built. Regard the description of Tardebigge Old Wharf on the Worcester & Birmingham canal in 1807 where, it was said, *". . . a commodious Bason, Wharf, Weighing Machine are prepared . . . to accommodate the numerous vessels passing through the canal . . . is most advantageously situated for trade, as the numerous warehouses, graneries, &c. &c. testify which have been erected here".*

New towns were built at the river or sea outlets of waterways where transhipment was necessary from barges, coasters or deep sea ships, which in their turn

Complexity in cranes — Sheffield & South Yorkshire Navigation, Rotherham

required a bason or haven to lie in while taking their place in the queue. Typical of these was Runcorn where *"Spacious wet docks and basins were constructed and a capacious warehouse built; but these accommodations were found to be insufficient for the requirements of the trade and the formation of additional locks and wet docks was determined upon in 1826 and completed in 1828"*. Even a relatively remote village could 'suffer' the effects of the new form of transport. A commentator of 1789 wrote, in praise of the Grand Trunk canal, "... the value of manufacturers arise in the most unthought of places; new buildings and new streets spring up in many parts of Staffordshire, where it passes; the poor no longer starving on the bread of poverty; and the rich grow greatly richer. The market town of Stone in particular soon felt this comfortable change; which from a poor insignificant place is now grown neat and handsome in its buildings, and from its wharfs and busy traffic, wears the lively aspect of a little sea port". Merthyr Tydvil owes almost its whole existance to the arrival of the Glamorganshire canal in 1794. "Merthyr Tydvil has lately been raised from a pretty village, to a town of some eminence by its forges of iron, mines of coal, and quarries of limestone, which have been rendered valuable by the canal extending from this inland place to Cardiff". Lechlade is now far from a bustling town and yet it once was claimed to be so having "the benefit of the canal between the Severn and the Thames . . . and both navigations make it a deposit for butter, cheese and other articles of inland trade".

Contiguous to this growth even non-canal ports and towns could find themselves in demand. Aberthaw, described as a small harbour and situated on the Welsh coast *"is only resorted to by a few coasting vessels of inferior burthen, for the purpose of conveying the produce of the district to other places, especially lias limestone, called Aberthaw tarras, which is much used in making cement for works under water, and for canal locks . . ."*, while the growth of transport meant new sources for basic materials became available, often to the villages' detriment. Aberdare, a hamlet in 1845, *". . . abounds with coal and iron-ore, the working of which . . . has materially defaced the beauty of the neighbourhood"* and worse, not only their eyes but pockets were despoiled by this new industry, *"The Aberdare canal, which is seven miles in length, communicates with the Glamorganshire canal, and, by means of a tram-road, with the extensive works at Hirwaun . . . the burthen of removals and accidents of a large proportion of the workmen falls upon the parish of Aberdare just within the limits of which their cottages are situated"*.

The traffics on waterways, at their prime, were not only the heavyweights — coal, iron, limestone or the like — but varied even to flannel. It was a great event on the Montgomeryshire canal when at Guilsfield a manufactory for this was opened and a branch of the canal was "built within half-a-mile of the village . . . at the expense of £2,000!". It would be tedious to detail all the items that were carried but salt was as important as coal; flour and wheat as vital as lime and without timber no boats would have been built. Oddments, but all bringing in butter to go with the shareholders' bread, included fruit, beans, peas, sugar, hams, cider, bark, potatoes, cheese, rapeseed, bricks, lead, gunpowder, soap, salt-scrow, dust and rags. Hemp was another load — discharged on occasion at a

Floating crane bereft of boiler, North Walsham & Dilham Canal

'Tyburn Wharf'! More odiferous cargoes, dung, night-soil, tanners' bark were singularly unremunerative for virtually all acts included a clause to the effect that these and other manures *"for the Improvement of Lands"* were to pass free of toll. To the long-suffering lock-keeper at Burscough on the Leeds & Liverpool canal, who had a boat load of night-soil sink in his lock, this must have added insult to injury!

After the canal was open steps had to be taken to procure an adequate number of boats, toll-keepers and, not least, boatmen — and what a bunch of scallywags these could be!

Whether or not boatmen were gypsies, vagabonds, ex-miners or whatever, when various waterways were first opened they had to be trained. It is hardly surprising that one of the first waterways, the Birmingham, was particularly hard hit. In 1769 an officer was despatched post-haste to Broseley and Madeley Wood on the River Severn *"to endeavour to procure two proper persons to steer . . . the Company's Boats"*, and five days afterwards the Secretary was instructed to write to John Gilbert, Agent to the Duke of Bridgewater, in order to borrow *"a Boy or two to steer the Boats"*.

Horses, too, were in very short supply — here the company required "sturdy beasts of good character" a phrase similar to that they had utilised when advertising for navvies! Unfortunately the animals they required were also in great demand by teamsters who wished to move wagon-loads of coal away from the wharfs. In 1770 a local newspaper whilst carrying an advertisement from the Birmingham Boat Company to the effect that coal was available at *"Four-pence per Hundred Weight"* and that *"Teams may depend on a constant Supply"* added a footnote: *"N.B. Wanted some careful able Men to unload the Boats; any such willing to engage are desired to apply at the Sign of the Nagg's Head on Snow-Hill in Birmingham. . . . The Wages will be Ten Shillings per Week"*.

Boats too, had to be obtained — at a cost in 1820 of £20 apiece; these were not the steel cabin boats that are now regarded as the epitome of narrow carrying but simple wooden structures, straight of side and bottom, terminating in a virtually upright bow and stern, identical save that for some unknown historical reason the steering platform at one end was always 4 inches higher than the other — despite the fact that these boats were designed to work from either end.

It was only as traffic began to move that the companies realised exactly what tartars they had caught with their boatmen. The basic carrying method was for the company owning a particular canal to operate their own boats, often, to avoid legal difficulties, under an alias (Trent & Mersey canal, Hugh Henshall & Co.; Birmingham canal, Birmingham Boat Company; Mersey & Irwell navigation, Old Quay Company) which in effect gave them a monopoly. The Trustees of the Bridgewater canal, by operating a closed shop, brought the coming of the Liverpool & Manchester Railway forward by a decade or so, but in the midlands independent carriers were soon to spring into being.

Leeds & Liverpool Canal, Leeds

Initially, boatmen were paid a flat wage, but this was fairly quickly changed to a system whereby they were paid by the trip. In 1780 the Birmingham canal advertised that a 'Weighing Machine' was in use, thus enabling the weight of cargo (the boats' weight was already registered) to be gauged and tolls charged accordingly. On the Thames & Severn canal at Briscombe Port a weigh-dock was built wherein the boat was weighed bodily. In the first year of use the Company was virtually paid in extra tolls the £1,062 it had cost. These docks were often very impressive structures, adding to, rather than distracting from, the local architectural scene. Braunston Junction caught the eye of a passerby who described the whole as *"Very interesting and rather singular; the weighing machine on one side and a lock-house on the other, are backed by a noble wood . . . the weighing-house steam engine, bridge lock and other objects make up a pretty scene".*

From the commencement of a trip too many men with mortal failings were involved and it seemed to take the canal companies quite a long time to undertake preventive measures against the men responding to temptation. Taking a normal coal run, robbery could start with the loader at the pit who in collusion with the boatman would forget to load a ton or two, the cargo being wetted to make up the weight difference. 'Fiddles' en route were as numerous as the boatmen themselves; toll-clerks, too, assuming they used coal fires, were not above issuing 'heavy-weight' tickets showing, say, 22½ instead of 20½ tons. On the journey the boatman (perhaps innocently) was open to the attentions of vagabonds, rogues and vagrant Irish; 'Peelers' not being invented until 1829 there was singularly little law enforcement. These *"rioters and thieves"* might be driven to stealing by hunger. In 1800 the harvest failed in Scotland and it was decided, in order to retain the navvies, to buy 100 quarter of oats or barley from London for the workmen on the Crinan canal, but in the Midlands the 'mob' were left to fend for themselves and, inter alia, in April of the same year *"they found their way to Nine Locks, Brierly Hill, and there took possession of two canal boats laden with grain for Birmingham".*

Even when the boat was to discharge, when weighing machines were brought into use — from about 1800 — any bagged goods had to be hung on a 'clicker' or counter. The tallyman's attention could be easily distracted and how those numbers could fly round when assisted by a judicious boot on the hanging bag! Coal was rarely weighed out, the toll clerks' ticket being taken as Gospel!

Sometimes boatmen got dragged into quarrels not of their making. One Monday, 13th December, 1830, the Reverend Skinner, looking out of his study window saw a mob proceeding to the coalpits at Camerton (Somerset Coal canal) and wrote in his diary, *"I walked thither . . . [and] The people at the pit said they were well satisfied with their wages . . . I counselled them against cutting the ropes of the pits and the damaging of machinery, etc., and advised them to return to their duty: that there were barges then waiting for their loads. The men said they would load the barges, and should not stop work: that they had nothing to complain of, only that they thought the small coal landed ought to be paid for as well as the large coal, since they procured one as well as the other"*. A common grievance this, as Somerset coal has long been known for easily breaking and there were not the outlets for slack that were to be found in the Midlands, where all coal represented *"black diamonds"*.

Even when boatmen were conspicuous by their absence, canal company employees stood in some risk of their belongings if not their lives. On the Birmingham canal at Smethwick on 21st December, 1789, John Bull, a company engineer who lived in the lockhouse was woken up by *"a violent wrenching of the house doors, and a battering of the walls"*. Getting up, he opened a window whereupon a large brick was thrown at him followed by thirteen other pieces of brick and stone, the men then broke in, ransacked the lower rooms and, forcing open the bedroom door, *"approached him, with pistols and iron-bars in their hands. . . . They compelled Mr. and Mrs. Bull to stand with their faces to the wall while they broke open a bureau, and stripped the room of everything they could carry away, the bed-clothes, &c. not excepted"*. So aggrieved were the Company at this that they offered a fifty guineas (£52.50) reward (when labourers wages were 50p a week) and not unsurprisingly three men were subsequently arrested and paid the ultimate penalty on the gallows.

Congestion on waterways was often aided and abetted by the boatmen, obviously a man working back 'light', or waiting to load, who, neither occupation being paid, was disinclined to give way to other boats. This accepted, the chaos that could occur in the candlelit stygian gloom of the limestone workings in the middle of the Dudley tunnel can be imagined. Some 3,172 yards (2,900 m) long, despite a hole in the middle, it was said of this: *"Deeply sunken amid rocks and caves, the sunbeam seldom warms its sullen waters; and the pallid beings who are occasionally seen propelling boats into the apertures of invisible passages, clad in their barracan mine dresses, cameleon like, appear to derive their hue from the rocks which surround them"*. Earlier it had been claimed that boats were delayed *"By empty Limestone Boats being left afloat* [i.e. unsecured] *in the Tunnel and By Boats Loaded with Limestone being left in the Canal. . . ."*. This problem was resolved by judicial means some thirty years later when a number of men were fined for infringing the canal company's byelaws. Another labour saving racket was worked by linking several boats together and employing only two men to work them, in lieu of the statutory requirement that two men should work each. This delayed the passage of passing boats, but meant the 'spare' men could be loading others. This, too, was resolved by similar means.

As independent carrying companies increased so did the number of boatmen, and more vociferous grew the complaints of shippers who had had goods purloined, for carriers like Albert Wood of Manchester carefully disclaimed responsibility for the loss of, or even damage to, some forty items including *"money, silver plate, glass, china, silk, furniture, paintings and wearing apparel"*; although he was prepared to insure them at the rate of 10p for £10 value. Under no circumstances would he worry about *"Aquafortis, Oil of Vitriol, or any other Ardent [fiery] spirits or Dangerous Articles"*, rather the consignor was liable to pay him for any damage these substances might cause to his boats. After excluding loss or damage caused by "Fire, Flood, Acts of God or Civil Commotion" whether the goods were on boats, wharves or wherever, some 900 words or so later on in the contract another clause clearly stipulates *"Also that he [Albert Wood] shall NOT be held liable in case of Strike, Combinations of Workmen, Storms, Floods, Fogs or Frosts in Rivers or Canals"*.

It is not known who developed the idea of 'locked' boats, but these gradually became more common. Basically the bulk of the boat was boxed in, with hatches for loading and discharging of goods, akin to the hold of a sailing ship. Advertisements from about 1800 onward speak of these being in use, initially for specific loads. Crowley, Leyland & Hicklin, after mentioning they carried from the Crescent Wharf, Birmingham, added as an afterthought *"N.B. Wines and spirits are conveyed in boats secured by locks"*. More general usage followed and although a slightly increased rate was charged this was balanced by lower insurance premiums.

A further development in the early 1800s was through carriage of goods *"in one bottom"*, offered by, among others, Martin Keddy who carried from Ripon to Hull twice a week, and from 1810 Crocket & Salkeld who, operating from Birmingham, proudly stated *"No other firm conveys goods all the way to Liverpool by their own vessels"*. This in itself a radical change from the shorthaul days where goods were trans-shipped at the end of a day's run, as while journeys of great distances were advertised, naturally including "all intermediate places" — Liverpool to Bristol (Robert Marshall); Worcester to Gainsborough (John Danks); Congleton to Uxbridge (T & W Ebbern); London to Manchester (Antwis & Sturland); Burton-upon-Trent to Scarborough (Joseph Smith & Sons) — generally four or five carriers would be involved. Although trans-shipment added materially to costs, the problem for the small carrier was that internecine competition, and a surprising lack of movement of long haul, heavy goods in the UK mainland, mitigated against his getting a full, economic (20-ton) load. A further snag was that most canal companies had a byelaw, designed to preserve water supplies that stipulated *"Barges or other Vessels passing through a Lock, or Locks, not carrying Twenty Tons, to pay for Twenty Tons"* or something similar, a strong discouragement to these undercapitalised firms as very few of the services offered were operated by other than loose partnerships, sharing booking agents and warehouse facilities.

The notable exception was Pickfords, who by reason of their already extant road carrying had no difficulty in applying their organisation and methods to the 'Water Turnpike'. At their peak they had 116 boats and 398 horses wholly owned and many on charter. Few complaints appear to have been received about their men or services. But this was hardly true of East Anglian 'Turnpike Sailors'

Surrey Docks, c.1890

who, when their waterways were frozen over, went 'on the tramp' committing various acts of mayhem. One offered a woman at a lonely cottage a number of new-fangled 'Californian' candles which he swore would light up the whole house. After selling her a few he went off, warning her to be careful and they would last her the whole winter. She lit one and popped out of the door, returning to find, truly, that the whole house was indeed lit. The 'Californian' candles were, it seems, made from pitch and tar with red ochre for colouring and a twist of oakum for a wick; all items normally carried on Fen lighters for 'patching and pithering' when laid up.

Occasionally the biter was bit, for example when having craftily half-filled their boat with water and slipped under the shutter (which theoretically barred access) at a copper works and 'gained' a few hundredweight of ingots, two rather dim individuals did not immediately make their way off at great speed but merely backed out, tied up and went to the local hostelry. When they awoke in the morning they meekly surrendered and received seven years penal servitude apiece.

During the building of the Caledonian canal it was considered reasonable by the proprietors to establish a small brewery at Corpach in order to *"induce the workmen to relinquish the pernicious habit of drinking whiskey"* but as middle-age approached on the Forth & Clyde canal the company, rather spitefully one feels, insisted that any employees who refused to give up *"the habit of intoxicating themselves occasionally"* should be *"forthwith dismissed"*. Perhaps they had heard of people drowning themselves while under the influence — on the Worcester & Birmingham canal this was so common amongst leggers working boats through Tardebigge tunnel that the Earl of Plymouth rather autocratically closed one public house at Tardebigge and demolished another!

Drink has taken its toll of many canal users, typical of many reports is that relating to *"a young man named Butters"* who was found *"floating on a balk of timber on the Liskeard Canal, being rather intoxicated he fell into the water and was drowned"*; while on the Somerset Coal canal the local vicar duly recorded in 1803 that *"Culling Macnam . . . being much intoxicated on Saturday night was drowned by falling into the Canal"*. Gloomily, one has to confess that still, deep, water has a fascination for suicides, and the same cleric was disturbed again when a *"servant knocked at the door and informed me that Lockyear's wife had drowned herself in the Canal"*. Mayhem was sometimes suspected, the Reverend Skinner, an asiduous diarist, added after yet another drowning *". . . appearances were so singular as to induce some to suppose it was not accidental, but God knows"*. The Coroner gave a very noncommital verdict — *"Found drowned"*.

Even a purely accidental drowning on the Caledonian canal aroused little pity in the authorities who, when a lock-keeper of forty years service was drowned in a lock, decided that because of the precarious state of their finances they could not assume any 'permanent burden' for his widow and child but gave her instead "a gratuity of £10" immediately after they had evicted them from their home. The church in Scotland was not happy either, the Reverend Andrew Sym of Kilpatrick formally complaining to the Directors of the Forth & Clyde canal that the funeral expenses of people drowned in the canal were seriously reducing his parish funds.

The use of towpaths by animals including *"every Horse, Mare, Gelding, Mule or Ass, not hailing or drawing any boat, barge or other Vessel, nor going from Field to Field or to or from Water or Pasture"* were strictly governed with tolls chargeable; drovers en route to market often finding this route kinder to the animals feet. Without doubt the proprietors of various navigations gnashed their collective teeth when, as an act of lese-majeste, their channel was mis-used for the purposes of skating. *"As it had frozen hard during the night and the boys wished me to accompany them to skaite, I walked with them to the Dundas Aqueduct in Claverton valley, and skaited for four hours on a fine piece of ice where the Combe Hay canal had not been broken. Some of the Catholic gentlemen from Downside passed us, and said they had come on the canal the whole way from Camerton"*. Having no other income when the boats were frozen in, one imagines the Secretaries feverishly searching through their Acts to see which rate was applicable.

6 THE VICTORIAN AGE

The total tonnage that was moved by boats on the inland waterways during the 19th century will never be precisely known unless a statistician has the endless time and boundless energy to tot up all the figures, but statistics made available by Board of Trade returns indicate roughly 40 million tons were waterborne in 1838, of which about a quarter was carried on family-crewed boats.

It is not known who first introduced the general principle of 'family' boats; while in general prior to 1830 the bulk of carriers used daymen, there are innumerable instances of families being aboard — in the summer there are many worse ways of living than on a boat! Heating and lighting costs were minimal, many a pheasant, hare or rabbit went towards the food bill, while the wife's labour helped speed up journey times, which in turn meant a greater income.

By 1835 though the principle of the wife living aboard was accepted; as manpower for maintenance was cut so were boatmen's wages. The twin evils of 'trip-money' and the 'Tommy Shop' came and stayed, the former to the end of carrying on narrow canals, the latter, in a modified form, even until the 1950s. The bulk of day-boatmen lived, as did most of the population, in a tied cottage; it was no problem for the employer to either raise the rent, or eject the boatman, offering as a substitute the boat's cabin, and it must be mentioned here that only the 'Captain', or steerer, of the boat was paid, for all that, in later days, the wife not only steered the butty and looked after the children but was also the cook/skivvy combined. A propos of tied cottages, rather anachronistically, the British Waterways Board, even today, retain a good number of these, and many a man tempted to raise some matter in dispute has gone away muttering after a timely reminder of his subservient condition.

The majority of canals were described at the Royal Society of Arts Conference in 1888 as remaining *"the enlarged mud-ditches of the last century, though now very much out of repair and half silted up. The old and obsolete systems of working and management are still in force. . . . Engineering improvements have been neglected, so that the old difficulties to through-traffic, caused by variety in the width of locks and depth of canals (entailing heavy costs in transhipment and delay) still exist under the divided interests of small local companies"*.

In truth the bulk of traffic remained in the holds of the orthodox boats, horse-drawn and on narrow (plus, here and there, wide) waterways, with the boatman

Family boats at rest, c.1952

and his family as crew, nevertheless the popular Victorian belief fostered by some of the traffics carried was that the boat was *"Scarcely fit to be used; old and worn out, leaky, never painted or well cleaned for years (beyond an occasional fumigation) and consequently filthy beyond description"*; the horse *"as a rule, in the last stages of decay, and more fit for the knackers yard than for work"*; and the boatmen *"a race of beings who are now living in pretty nearly the same condition as did the people of the Bronze Age"*.

The full saga of boat-people has been written elsewhere but one aspect often overlooked is that even until the 1930s congestion at locks was a cause of much aggravation and the resulting scraps went a long way towards making the boatman's black reputation.

Farmers' Bridge Locks, in the heart of the Birmingham Canal Navigations, provided, in 1839, the only sensible link between the Trent & Mersey via the Main Line and the Oxford, Coventry and Birmingham & Fazeley canals. Despite the fact that they were open round the clock and also (horror) upon Sundays some 'Branches of Trade' had to be diverted to other longer routes as *"the pressure* upon them during the Autumnal and Winter months is excessive, from Twenty to Thirty Boats being frequently found at the top, and as many at the bottom of the Locks, waiting for a passage". Not only were family boats affected here but also the day-boatmen. "The lives of the men who work the 'open boats' appears to be still more comfortless; they have no shelter, and often sleep, say one night, on board, doing the best they can. Their fire is a huge open, circular grate, such as we see at night on roads under repair, and it seems to me that the approved mode of taking a siester [sic] is to lie flat on the back, with boots as near the fire as may be convenient. Being, at least for a time, bachelors, the crews of the open boats appear to be more morose and dissatisfied than their brethren in the cabins. We come on a great fleet of these boats, waiting their turns at a tedious 'block' at one of the locks; some of the unfortunates have been there an hour, and have every prospect of waiting another hour; darkness is coming on, and the night is intensely cold".

Hours became longer as wages fell, until in the 1870s 5 a.m. to 8 p.m. was normal, Sunday included, but partly due to pride, and partly because of an inate decency, little complaint was made. "The children are far from uncouth in manner, and the mother is kindly and frank of speech. Like most of her class, she was a boatman's daughter, and has known no other phase of existence. She does not complain of boat-life 'when you 'as yer 'ealth' but opines that 'it's bitter bad in sickness'. No school, and no church for this family, unfortunately, for the boat is loaded, and leaves at daybreak. We put some jocular questions on the subject of aquatic courtship and matrimony. 'Oh, yes', she laughingly admits, 'Young fellers goes a coortin' to the boats, married into the boats, and does the best they can'. I learn that the wedding feasts on board are of the most jovial character. But this is a bright picture of canal life . . .". When complaint was made, nostalgia was uppermost, ". . . there was a time when they were better off, and when they went into a public-house to have a glass of grog they were put into the parlour. Now they are kicked and cuffed about anywhere, and put in any dirty hole out of sight, and the drink they get is not of the best sort".

It is regrettable that the image of canals today is, misleadingly, of a serene, green water-road — although this is better than that of the late 19th century when all waterways were firmly believed to be similar to Sir Nigel Gresley's waterway from Newcastle to Stoke-on-Trent. ". . . the water in it was inky black, and the stench intolerable. Large bubbles of gas were continually rising to the surface, being unmistakable proof of decomposing animal and vegetable matter. Three or four drains were running into it, and the carcases of several dogs in various stages of decomposition floating about".

Generally, Victorian commentators studiously avoided mentioning one traffic which had to go by boat which must surely have exposed the boatman concerned to every virus, bug or germ as ever was. A boatman was asked, "Do you carry night-soil [contents of privies, cess-pools, etc.]?", and he, without apparent disgust, answered, "We have one place to which we can carry it, over the canal-bridge, about 500 yards on the same road. We lay it there in the midst of a very large field; the person who allows us the privilege of shooting it there (Mr. Clarke) bakes it, I believe, and sends it over to the West Indies . . .". The question then arose regarding the disposal of offal, road-sweepings, and general city refuse. "Our general plan is to contract; we

74

Farmers Bridge Locks — once the scene of congestion

underlet our work of sifting to a man, and we give him everything that it produces except the ashes and breeze. He gets the rags and bones and other things. The oyster-shells belong to us, he sells the bones. . . . The bones are always sold to the Jews; and they send them away in barges, and they are taken and boiled, I believe, in the country somewhere, and ground and used as bone-dust for manure. . . . The woollen coarse rags are taken into the country and laid down till they moulder away, and then the rag-dust is sold to the hop-farmers in Kent. It is a most excellent thing to prevent the fly in wine. Oyster-shells, broken crockery ware, and everything that we call 'hard-core' is sold to the contractors for roads . . . there is no better thing in existence. . . .''

Looking at the clean domestic waste of today this might not seem too bad a job, and unlikely to affect the men, but regard the state of another, but similar, dungheap from which the produce was boated away. *"The effluvia all round about this place in summer is horrible. There is a land of houses adjoining, four stories in height, and in the summer each house swarms with myriads of flies; every article of food and drink must be covered, otherwise, if left exposed for a minute, the flies immediately attack it, and it is rendered unfit for use, from the strong taste of the dunghill left by the flies".*

A commentator, George Smith, watched, probably in horror, when he saw between the Bishop's Road Bridge and the South Wharf, Paddington *"some 100 to 150 women and children scratching among the ashes and filth of London to find bits of leather, rags, old bones, and other refuse, and loading them in boats, and the rest that was not worth sending away was burnt on the spot. On the other side were to be seen boats laden with all kinds of manure, smoking and stinking on a hot summer's day; the boaters evidently enjoying it as pigs would on a dung heap; and for nearly half a mile you could hardly put your foot down without setting it in filth; all this is taking place within a stone's throw of 'fashionable Paddington'''.*

Day boatman, Birmingham Canal Navigation, main line

"When you 'as yer 'ealth"

As might be expected on the boats employed on this trade, bugs abounded, but unlike a house a boat could be (more or less thoroughly) fumigated with brimstone — an occupation nicknamed 'bug-chasing' as *"yer chased 'em aht the cabin inter the 'old and when yer'd done they chased you ahter the cabin back onto the bank!"*.

Whether irritated or amused at the condescension of a writer in 1878 who expressed surprise at seeing *"a boat the other day, named 'Buy your own Cherries'. Both the boater and his wife and all the children were thoroughly clean and respectable looking, and neither swearing nor drunkenness were seen or heard on board the boat, and nearly all the children could read and write"*, nevertheless it is much more pleasant to read a 'write-up' of some Northern boatmen in 1859, which by itself gives many a clue to how the accepted characteristics of men who lived or worked on canals were developed:
"The Keelmen are a hardy and a laborious class of men, and are distinguished for their great muscular strength. Few employments require greater exertion than theirs, nor could they perform it were they not supported by nutritious food. Accordingly, the hardy keelman never goes aboard the keel till his basket is stored with best flour, which, with a bottle of beer, form his usual diet. The flesh, which is of the fattest kind, is sliced, laid upon a piece of bread, and then cut into convenient bites with a knife. Seated around the huddock or cabin of the keel, and covered with perspiration and coal-dust, they enjoy their meal with peculiar cheerfulness. One boy is attached to every keel, and he is under the immediate orders of the skipper (the chief per-

son on board); but each of the keel's crew contributes a small portion of his victuals for the boy's support while aboard. From the practice of hailing one another on the river, especially during the night-time, they acquire a loud and vociferous manner of expressing themselves; yet their conduct is uniformly civil and exemplary, and they are gradually losing the blunt roughness by which they have been characterised. They are remarkably friendly to each other, being all keel-bullies, or keel-brothers".

These were the types of men who manned our coasters and who, in desperation, driven from waterways by poor trade, served us well in the Royal Navy; it is ironic that these 'mud-hoppers', 'sewer-rats', 'reed-buntings' or 'water gypsies' were regarded as suitable 'Ambassadors of the Crown' to *"the Kaffir of South Africa, the negro of the Coromandel sea-board, the savage Malay, and the cannibal islanders of the Great South Sea".*

From the 1850s onwards various well-meaning if misguided 'do-gooders' attempted to turn the boatman to Christianity; describing themselves as 'missionaries', they went about their task much as they did in the wilds of Africa and to judge by their attitudes were equally fearful of encountering cannibals, wild tribal dances and 'yellow jack'.

At the time of the Great Exhibition the plight of the men employed on the oldest navigation in England, the Thames, was becoming desperate. Not long ago the Queen's watermen had been *"proprietors of lighters and prosperous"*, assisted by exemption from taxes, but their number had dwindled and only four 'hog-grubbers', ex-naval men, who plied for hire from *"the Pelican Stairs"* remained. *"There was from forty to fifty of them, sir, . . . when I was a lad, and I am not fifty-three, and fine old fellows they were. But they're all going to nothing now"*. The laws of the river stated that a waterman had to serve a seven year apprenticeship but *"There's a good many from Rochester way, sir* [one waterman said in 1850] *and down that way. They've got in through the interest of members of Parliament, and suchlike, while there's many free watermen, that's gone to the expense of taking up their freedom, just starving. But we are going to see about it, and it's high time. Either give us back the money we've paid for our rights, or let us have our proper rights — that's what I say"*. In fact the day of the waterman was, to all intents and purposes, over, as omnibuses and steamers took away their trade — sadly they realised this all too well. *"I remember the first steamer on the river; it was from Gravesend, I think. It was good for us men at first, as the passengers came ashore in boats. There was no steam-piers then, but now the big foreign steamers can come alongside, and ladies and cattle and all can step ashore on platforms. The good times is over, and we are ready now to snap at one another for 3d* [1p] *when once we didn't care about 1s.* [5p]. *We're beaten by engines and steamings that nobody can well understand, and wheels".*

7

THE AGE OF CHANGE

The total sum invested in canal building has never been accurately computed but a figure of £32 million spread over fifty years is probably a reasonable estimate; by contrast in 1846, 14 years after the opening of the Liverpool & Manchester railway no less than £146 million was already, hopefully, bringing massive dividends nearer for railway companies, or over four and a half times more than the total expended on waterways. Transport events during the two decades 1830-1850 show that there was a remarkable state of flux, for this was the time when the rail and canal schemes overlapped.

The Liskeard & Looe canal was opened in 1831, the Birmingham & Liverpool Junction canal, which cut the journey time by boat from London to Liverpool from 7 to 5 days, was brought into use in 1834 and, rather oddly, the Chard — a lost cause if ever there was — received its Act the same year. Two years later the Croydon canal was closed but to balance this the Aire & Calder introduced steam tugs for the haulage of barges. By 1846, 853 miles (1372 km) of canal had fallen into the hands of railway interests and as the railway 'mania' gained strength within the following five years (1847-1852) another 203½ miles lost their independence. Not perhaps a vast mileage out of the total, but they included strategically vital waterways, effectively destroying the cohesion of the network. Perhaps the Fossdyke, Witham or Grantham were relatively unimportant, certainly the Oakham, Louth and Glastonbury had little value, but the loss of the Trent & Mersey, Shropshire Union network and the Kennet & Avon to all intents and purposes blocked the routes from London to Liverpool and Bristol.

Writing the story of the vicissitudes of canals from 1830 to the Manchester Ship Canal Act of 1886 can best be compared to a kitten trying to disentangle a skein of wool! So for simplicity, let us briefly look at the varied fortunes of four — a doomed late-comer, the Chard, lurking in Somerset; the Kennet & Avon, even today endeavouring to patch up the results of railway ownership; the Worcester & Birmingham which by becoming part of a waterway consortium competed with railways to some extent successfully, and the Aire & Calder, giant among pygmies.

The Chard suffered from a number of fundamental and inherent difficulties. In 1821 James Green, a visionary engineer too early for his time, surveyed the

Road Bridge at Wrantage, 1966

line of a canal to leave the abortive Bridgewater & Taunton near Taunton to Beer in Devon, which would have involved five inclined planes, three tunnels and a terminal basin, the whole canal being *"... on a very small scale, on which boats or four or five tons may be navigated in sets of four, six or eight boats, drawn by one Horse on the level Ponds of Canal, and passed singly up and down inclined planes by the aid of water Machinery, instead of locks ..."*. This was lost in the plans for a 200-ton ship canal, the English & Bristol Channels, which received its Act in 1825, but despite promising dividends of 12% on an expenditure of £1¾ million, in its turn it died away.

Out of the fraças came another request in 1830 to Green for a further survey, this time for a canal from Chard to the Bridgewater & Taunton canal. He recommended a railway. Once again he was approached, in 1833, to make another survey with instructions that it must be a canal, and he responded by suggesting £57,000 be expended on 13½ miles of waterway, involving two counterbalanced lifts and two inclined planes to gain the 200′ rise between the Bridgewater & Taunton canal at Creech St. Michael and Chard town basin, plus three tunnels requiring a total of some 2,475 yards (2263 m) of burrowing. Except for the substitution of Green by Sir William Cubitt and inclined planes for lifts, the work was carried out to plan, being opened in 1842 at a cost roughly double the estimate. Not, according to the local paper with much jubilation.

"*A few lines will suffice to announce the opening of this canal. This anxiously looked for event took place, quite accidentally, on the Queen's birthday. We say accidentally because, with the uncertain machinery at the inclined plane, and the celebrated frail rope, it was deemed a moral impossibility to say on what precise day any cargo could be brought to the wharfs. . . . The actual opening and celebration lasted but a few short hours. The ringers (who were about to let down the bells after ringing for Her Majesty) gave an additional peal or two by desire . . . .*"

Although one commentator writing a little later of his youth tells us: "*Merchants came with the canal in 1842. From out the new-made tunnel, at the head of the incline, barges appeared midst the playing of bands and shoutings of 'Rule Britannia' on the opening day, a memorable aquatic procession, and where now is a row of cottages, wharfage invited traders. The scene was a busy one: merchants set up: Giles & Thomas Lang were straight in their dealings, kind to poor neighbours, and prospered in limes and manures, over the West Country . . . .*"

Whatever the start, one prefers to think of the latter report, when by 1853, far from paying a 12% dividend as was hopefully planned, a receiver was installed as even interest on borrowed money was not being paid. In 1867, 37 years after Green had first suggested a railway was sensible, the shareholders — or perhaps the mortgagees — of the canal were pleased to recover around £6,000 from the Bristol & Exeter railway in exchange for their moribund concern.

The Kennet & Avon differs in many ways from the orthodox narrow canal. Engineered by Rennie, it consists of an artificial cut connecting with, and incor-

Steam tug and train of pans leaving Castleford bound for Goole, c.1920

Redundant barge at Dundas Aqueduct, 1960, Kennet & Avon Canal

porating, two river navigations, giving a through barge route from Bristol to the Thames.

The actual canal received its Act in 1794, and was after many vicissitudes completed in 1810. The original estimate of building costs was £214,000 although the final expenditure to the time of opening was not far short of £1 million. The reasons for this were a mixture of the usual, including inflation, changes of route and poor supervision, plus the unorthodox. A Prospectus of December 1790 extolled the virtues of this 'Western Canal' and . . . the disadvantages felt by sailing craft! *"In time of Peace, the Tediousness and Dangers of a coasting Voyage from Bristol, round the Land's End . . . to The Mouth of the Thames, and up that River to London, are extremely detrimental to the general Convenience of Trade. It has been asserted, that this circuitous Navigation, which requires a wind from most points of the Compass, employs as much time as an ordinary voyage to the West Indies. — In Time of War, when the Channel is full of Privateers, and when seamen are wanted for the Navy, an Inland Navigation from Bristol to London must be of the greatest national importance to our home and probably our West India Trade, and many other foreign Productions. . . ."*

By 1792 the mania was in full swing and amazing scenes occurred, none more so than on the proposals for this canal when *"people struggled violently with each other*

Tardebigge locks, reservoir to the left

in their rush to the subscription book . . . 10 guineas were paid for a Post Chaise from Bristol to Bath . . . and beds were charged at 1 guinea each!" As a labourer's wages were 40p for a 60 hour week such a price for a hotel bed was indeed amazing, equating to £100 in the values of 1977!

By 1793 plans were a little more settled and Rennie could promise completion *"within two years of the commencement of work"*, although the estimate had risen to £336,000, but it was not until 12th June 1797 that the first six-mile portion was opened from Newbury to Kintbury when:

"A barge of nearly 60 tons, having on board the band of the 15th Regiment of Dragoons, then stationed in Newbury, left that place at twelve o'clock and arriving at Kintbury at half-past two, where the Committee of the Canal, having dined with their Chairman, Mr. Charles Dundas, embarked at six o'clock and arrived at Newbury about half-past nine, the passage of the party affording great interest to a large number of persons assembled at different points on the route".

Great Bedwyn was reached two years later "when a barge of 50 tons, laden with coal and deals" was received "with great demonstrations of joy", a hardly surprising event as barrels of beer were provided for the navvies! By 1803 the canal was already falling to pieces simply because unseasoned Bath stone was used, against Rennie's advice, in lieu of bricks — *"Seeing the great Loss that the Company have sustained and the great detention which the Works have experienced from the badness of the Stone, I feel it my duty to repeat again to the Committee, what I have frequently done before, the propriety of again considering whether it would not be better to use Bricks generally, instead of Stone in the Works which are yet to do".*

The reason for making use of this obviously unsatisfactory material made

83

sense on the one hand, and yet was comical. The Proprietors of the Navigation hoped to develop a trade in Bath stone to London, much as granite was brought from Derbyshire via the Cromford canal, and could not afford to upset the quarry-owners. On the other hand it cost them about £75,000 in extra labour and materials carrying out repairs and delayed the opening of the waterway so, on balance, they were probably out of pocket.

By 1805 though, the casual observer might well presume the whole line were open, a carrier's advertisement reading:

"LONDON, BRISTOL AND READING

RIVER KENNET

and KENNET and AVON CANAL

WHITE and BARNARDS

NUMEROUS errors having lately occurred by the delivery of Goods in London intended for WHITE and BARNARD's conveyance, they are under the necessity of respectfully soliciting the attention of their Friends and the Public *to particularly observe* that they take in and deliver goods by their Barges at no other Wharf but the KENNET WHARF, UPPER THAMES STREET, LONDON, and continue to forward them as usual to and from thence, and the under-mentioned places, with regularity and expedition:-

Reading	Devizes	Bath and ⎤
Newbury	Bradford	Bristol ⎦
Hungerford	Trowbridge	Wells
Great Bedwin	Frome	Taunton
Swindon	Calne	Bridgwater
Marlborough	Chippenham	Exeter

Damage or loss (except by Leakage or Fire) will be accounted for on all Goods properly packed and Directed".

The final completion of the route — it being opened to traffic on 31st December 1810 — was not overwell publicised but tonnage and income rose steadily until in 1829 the Kennet & Avon canal, which now incorporated both the Avon and Kennet navigations, was probably at its peak for efficiency; the 29 locks of

Gloucester Docks in their heyday, c.1835

the Caen Flight, Devizes, being lit by gas to allow night working of barges, thus easing congestion during the day. The official 'resolution' reads:

"*. . . no Barge or Boat be allowed to enter any one of the Devizes Locks after the Gas shall be lighted but on payment of one shilling for each Barge and six pence for each Boat which payment shall entitle the Owner to navigate his Barge or Boat through the said Locks so long as the Gas shall be lighted but no longer*", an encouragement to trade which would probably have annoyed William Cobbett greatly for, as he wrote in 1826, "*Devizes is, as nearly as possible, in the centre of the county and the canal, that passes close by it, is the great channel through which the produce of the country is carried away to be devoured by the idlers, the thieves, and the prostitutes, who are all tax-eaters, in the Wens of Bath and London*".

Twelve years later, on 30th June 1841, Brunel's Great Western railway was opened from Bristol to Bath with an immediate effect on the canal, receipts dropping from the £51,000 of 1840 by £11,000 in the following year.

Economies and toll reductions followed — a pattern repeated on virtually every other waterway faced with rail rivalry. By 1845 the Committee considered "*the expediency of converting the Canal into a Railway*", but after a survey and attempting to obtain an Act for this purpose the following year "*. . . they trust that as a General Meeting will shortly be held, the explanations which will there be given, of the arrangement come to with the G.W.R. Co., and the Wilts, Somerset & Weymouth Railway Co., will be satisfactory*". This agreement was not for the sale of the waterway but

The first tunnel in Bath, Kennet & Avon Canal

for compensation to be paid by the GWR for the withdrawal of the Bill; six years later the Proprietors of the Kennet & Avon canal were pleased to sell the whole waterway *"together with debts, contracts and liabilities"* to the GWR receiving in return an annual payment — the equivalent of a ¾% dividend!

The first change made by the GWR was the letting out on three-year agreements not only of maintenance but also lock-keeping to contractors — a throwback to the days shortly after the canal's opening. In no way could this work in the waterways' favour; maintenance had already been cut back in the 1842 economies when staff dropped by a fifth to 100 (for 106 miles — 171 km — and 86 locks); dredging, lock-repairs and towpath management were all, if not neglected, sketchily carried out. Far from the halcyon gas-lit days of 1829, in 1861 night-working (on the canal section) was prohibited, and following the move of the administrative staff from Bath to Paddington in 1862, boatmen were prohibited from having fires on boats — ostensibly because of the risk of a conflagration! By 1875 matters had reached such a pretty pass that one trader wrote to the Board of Trade, a so-called impartial body, claiming that "the Navigation of the Kennet and Avon Canal, has been allowed to fill up with Mud that Barges are obliged only to take on Board about thirty tons instead of fifty tons their proper freight . . .".

The Worcester & Birmingham, like the Chard, experimented with lifts, but decided for all their apparent value they were not as reliable as the traditional lock. The idea of the waterway started under a cloud, meeting with fierce and expensive opposition, but eventually got the 'go-ahead' in 1791, but subject to severe restrictions. Contention was fierce, one writer *"Not An Inhabitant of Birmingham"*, claimed:

"Birmingham, from its Advantage in Point of Situation, must always have command of the Coal Trade; and the Bowels of the Earth furnish inexhaustible Quantities of this valuable and necessary Article, which will always find its Way to Market, so long as the Price will pay for raising it, and a small profit to the Proprietor, which has not hitherto been the Case. It is surprising that a narrow and groundless Jealousy on this Head, so contrary to the liberal Spirit of an enlightened Age and Country, should at all interrupt a Scheme which would be the noblest Improvement ever attempted in this Town and Neighbourhood; which by extending the Conveniences of Traffic and Commerce, would necessarily extend the Trade, and increase the Riches and Consequence of this Country".

Water supply, compensation payments and greedy landlords took their toll, and as if that were not enough physical junction with the Birmingham Canal was prohibited — leading to the infamous 'Bar' whereover all goods had to be transshipped with the risk of damage and theft.

Fall Ings Lock, 1970

Briefly the canal mania had its effect: *"Navigation shares are so universally sought after that a holder of that kind of property may consider himself truly fortunate. Ten shares in the Birmingham and Worcester Canal were, on Wednesday last, sold by auction, by Mr. Boot, for a premium of two hundred and ninety-four pounds".*

The canal was built to take barges, the original plan being to allow through communication of Severn vessels to Birmingham, but despite having five engineers it took 16 years to complete the length from Birmingham to Tardebigge Old Wharf, some part of the time being lost cutting Wast Hill tunnel. *"April 10, 1797. This great tunnel is at length completed. The first brick of the stupendous work was laid on the 28th of July, 1794, and it was wholly arched over on the 25th of February, 1797. It is also worthy of remark, that Seventeen hundred and eighty-two yards, two feet, and eight inches, were finished from 1st January, 1796, to the 1st of January, 1797. At the commencement of this undertaking, the practicability of it was treated with the greatest ridicule and reprobation; it was said that the embankment and deep cutting, and the tunnel, could not be executed; we can, however, at this moment say, that by the great skill and attention of the Engineers, Messrs. Jones & Cartwright, the whole of this business is most substantially finished . . .".*

It was not until 1815 that the whole line to Worcester was opened, howbeit using narrow locks and thus precluding the use of river craft. Nevertheless it received a mention in the local newspaper: *"About half past 10 in the morning of that day [4th December 1815] several boats started from Tardebigge, and between 5 and 6 in the evening the first of them arrived at a wharf in Sidbury, adjoining this city. Several boats afterwards arrived; among others was one of Messrs. Pickfords' with a cargo from Manchester".*

The estimate was for a total expenditure of about £180,000, the actual outlay some £600,000, and it was six years after the opening (1821) that a first dividend of 1% was disgorged. Whether the delay in the building of the Gloucester & Berkeley (opened 1827) made much financial difference is speculative; already in 1825 the Worcester & Birmingham shareholders were jumpy, *". . . whether the Canal will be able to retain its trade amidst the many projects for conveying Goods on Railroads, time only can determine . . .".*

Fortunately, the 'Bar' in Birmingham had been removed in 1815 being replaced by a regulating lock, and this together with the growth of salt interests in Droitwich led to increased profits over the next decade or so, but in 1841 a sombre note appeared in the Company's records *". . . a considerable portion of those Goods and Merchandise which would otherwise have waited the breaking up of the frost and the re-opening of the Canal were during the continuation of the frost forwarded by the Railroad".* This was also the year in which the Birmingham & Gloucester railway was opened throughout, causing cuts in tolls, tonnage carried — and profits. Worse was to come for the Oxford, Worcester & Wolverhampton railway was approaching by 1851, and unusually for a canal company the Worcester & Birmingham sought to defend their trade firstly by promoting and, more or less, owning, a new waterway from the Droitwich Barge canal to their own and

Barges loaded, Aire & Calder Canal

then, by lease, took control of the relatively ancient (opened 1771) Droitwich canal itself, thus ensuring that, as far as possible, the salt traffic remained in their hands.

Not even this sufficed, so in the next decade they tried to sell themselves — outright or by lease — to the OWWR. (That failed and not for nothing this railway had the nickname "Old Worse & Worse"). They then tried the West Birmingham railway, and finally, the Midland. All failed and despite vast improvements in the salt trade by 1875 when *"there was ever greater pumping power at Stoke than at Droitwich. Four brine-pits were in use. Fifty canal boats, four hundred railway vans, were in the possession of Mr. Corbett, the owner of the saltworks. Five thousand, six hundred hands were employed in the industry after Mr. Corbett dispensed with women workers. The rate of production was about 3,000 tons a week . . ."*, the cost of maintenance far outstripped income.

One reason for the failure of the Worcester & Birmingham to either turn itself into a railway or to sell up was the steadfast opposition of the Gloucester & Berkeley Canal Company who needed the waterway as a feeder; and as the Severn had undergone numerous improvements they saw no reason why trade should not be increased. In 1873 the now grandiloquently entitled Sharpness New Docks Company (in reality the Gloucester & Berkeley Canal Company)

89

approached the Worcester & Birmingham to discuss a take-over; this being subsequently ratified by Parliament in 1874 — the holding company for the G & BCC, W & BCC, DCC and DJCC being thereafter the even more cumbersomely entitled Sharpness New Docks and Gloucester & Birmingham Navigation Company.

The Aire & Calder, that doyen of waterways then and now, was pursuing a very different course. Tonnage carried on the Kennet & Avon canal showed a steady decline from 360,610 tons of 1848, through 210,567 in 1858 to, in 1888, 135,802. The Aire & Calder, conversely, rose from 1,335,783 (1848) via 1,747,251 (1868) to, breaking the two million mark for the first time, 2,210,692 in 1888. By contrast, we can compare the Birmingham Canal Navigations at, roughly, 4, 7 and 7½ million tons, or the Pocklington at 8, 5½ and 1 thousand tons!

During the 1840s and 1850s the Aire & Calder had come to various traffic agreements with the railways which threatened its lifestream. These agreements certainly avoided the cut-throat toll cutting competition which developed elsewhere but nevertheless proved to work against the best interest of the waterway and by 1855 it was apparent that either sale of its property to the Lancashire & Yorkshire or the North Eastern railways or independents were the choices; and rather courageously — in view of a certain cut in dividends — the shareholders chose the latter.

Having leased the Barnsley canal in 1854, in 1863 they took over the Calder & Hebble for a 21 year period, followed by, purchasing jointly with the Leeds & Liverpool canal, the Bradford — described in 1861 as a *"3-miles long open, pestiferous sewer"*, seemingly unchanged from 1845 when an official report was scathing. *"The main sewers are discharged either into the brook or into the terminus of a canal which runs into the lower part of the town. The water of this basin is often so charged with decaying matter, that in the hot water bubbles of sulphurated hydrogen are continually rising to the surface . . . watch-cases and other materials of silver become black in the pockets of workmen employed near the canal. The stench is sometimes very strong and fevers prevail . . . ".* Closed for health reasons in 1867 it was re-opened in 1873 and staggered along until 1922 when financial and physical problems led to its final closure.

T.H. Bartholomew, engineer of the Aire & Calder, died in 1853 and was succeeded by his son William, possibly one of the most brilliant men to grace canals, and the leading exponent of improvements in boat working. Steamboats were tried on canals in the last quarter of the previous century, with varying degrees of success and in 1826, on 2nd October, *"A Steam Canal Boat arrived in this town* [Birmingham] *on Friday last, from London, carrying twenty tons, and is the first successful attempt ever made. . . . The result of this experiment has been perfectly satisfactory, and when the machinery is applied to regular canal boats of a suitable construction, it is calculated that one whole day will be saved in time between London and Birmingham. It is the intention of the proprietors to establish a line of steam boats immediately"*; although this was not followed up. In 1833 at least 20 steamers were operating from Hull to such diverse points

Barge loaded with 70 tons of coal on its way to Thornhill Power Station, Dewsbury, 1971

as London (coastwise), Barton, Selby, Gainsborough, Brigg and York, while the *"Steam towing boat, called the* Britannia *of fifty horse power is provided to facilitate the navigation of the Rivers Humber and Ouse. . . . The master of the* Britannia *is at all times ready to take charge of any vessel bound to Goole".*

Goole was an early development built by the Aire & Calder Navigation Company from a hamlet to a thriving sea-port, its seal of approval being given in 1828 when the 'Commissioners of His Majesty's Customs' had 'appointed' a part of the port of Goole as *"warehouses of special security, for the deposit of all articles except tobacco and snuff . . .",* thus enabling imported items to stay under bond, either for re-export or onward transmission. In addition to this the Aire & Calder had *"upwards of seven thousand superficial yards of vaults and floor, for the bonding of every description of goods and merchandize . . . another warehouse for the bonding of foreign grain, which comprises upwards of five thousand superficial yards of flooring . . . a pond for the reception of timber under bond, capable of receiving upwards of three thousand loads . . . a range of deal yards, fourteen in number; together with spacious sheds, and every other accommodation that modern ingenuity could devise . . .".*

Incidentally, by 1962 nine docks were in use, with a water area of 36¾ acres (1487 ares) and no less than three miles of quays handling 2530 vessels and, including exports of 1,794,028 tons (of which 1,545,668 tons were of coal) a total of just over 2¼ million tons of goods. Obviously, even in 1831, movements of boats had to be expedited above the pace of a horse and the use of a steam tug brought the journey times down to eight hours from Leeds to Goole and forty-five from Manchester, while an *"elegant steam packet"* conveyed passengers daily from Castleford to Goole.

As speed generated more traffic so the locks were lengthened and widened to allow *"the full benefits and economy of Steam Traffic [which] can only be realized by enabling a larger class of Vessels to proceed with their Cargoes as far as possible up the navigation and by means of increased facilities for the passage of trains of Boats drawn by a Tug".* By 1867 trains of orthodox barges — ten or more — towed by a tug were commonplace while steam 'flyboats' introduced at Bartholomew's suggestion in 1852, offered a quicker, if dearer, service for lighter or urgently needed goods.

In 1862, however, Bartholomew not only patented, but persuaded the Aire & Calder Navigation directors to give a trial to his Mk.I compartment boats. While the use of compartment boats, i.e. boxes within barges, was not new, what was unique was the suggestion that these boxes should dispense with the barge and operate much as a train of railway wagons, close coupled but pushed by a steam tug and controlled by means of, initially, chains, but latterly, wire ropes alternatively slackened and tightened on turns in the canal to give the necessary articulation. Together with the introduction of additional loading staithes or wharfs, built at the Company's expense against a guarantee of tonnage from the colliery owners, and hydraulic hoists at Goole whereby each compartment boat — or 'Tom Pudding' — was inverted and discharged through a shute into the waiting steamer; the Aire & Calder found itself by 1888 in a well-nigh unassailable position vis-a-vis railways. Bartholomew too, justly went from strength to strength, becoming general manager as well as engineer in 1876 and four years later Chairman of the Goole Steam Shipping Company. In 1896 he supervised the commencement of the building of the New Junction canal which provides a 5½ mile, singularly straight, connection between the River Dun (Shef-

Locking down into the River Ouse from Goole Docks, 1971

field & South Yorkshire Navigation) and the Aire & Calder — although technically at least he retired a year earlier! This waterway was completed in 1905, and Bartholomew busied himself with other waterway matters almost until his death in 1919 at the age of 88.

His Mk. I compartment boat system, pushing the 'pans', was superseded in the 1890s by a logical development whereby a tug pulled the 'pans', a 'Jebus', or false bow unit, breaking the water and allowing the propeller thrust to pass away cleanly. Spring buffers and a modified coupling eliminated the wire steering, and trains of 30 to 40 boats became commonplace; boats in use rising from 125 in 1877 to 401 (of a larger size) twenty years later.

Within papers read at the annual meetings of canal engineers interesting comparative figures on costs can be found. It was stated in 1895 that the *"floating tanks . . . hauled by a tug"* on the Aire & Calder, cost, for the return journey, 0.0036p per ton mile (i.e. to transport 100 tons for one mile cost ⅓rd of a penny) while cargo-carrying steamers cost 0.0125p, and horse-haulage 0.058 or, roughly, 15 times more expensive than a 'pan'. On the neighbouring Leeds & Liverpool canal, where the whole canal was smaller, and resistance to boat movements through the water higher, the cost rose to 0.1375p per ton per mile (i.e. 100 tons for one mile cost 13¾ pence). Small wonder therefore that the most 'alive' engineers sought to introduce steam haulage. Some railways prohibited steam boats, i.e. the Great Western railway, and thus waterways like the Kennet & Avon were to remain totally uncompetitive.

The reason behind this was, on the face of it, simple; that increased speed meant more wear and tear on the canal banks, engineering and maintenance costs rose, but tolls were limited by Parliament. This premise conveniently overlooks the fact that rising trade can increase toll revenue!

8

THE STEAM AGE

For fifty years or more prior to the Great War the threefold objectives of eliminating family boats, speeding up traffic and reducing the wear and tear on canal banks exercised the minds of the foremost canal engineers.

Initial experiments covered such matters as the shape of the hull and it was found that — for example — covering the hull with oil-cloth reduced resistance. Even the most compact engine necessarily meant a loss of tonnage capacity, possibly to an uneconomic level, and it was apparent therefore, despite the extra lockage, that a self-contained tug was the most advantageous method of mechanisation. But alternatives were propounded, as when Fowlers of Leeds, makers of steam traction engines and cable ploughs experimented at their expense with a system whereby the tug hauled itself along a cable or chain laid in the bottom of the waterway; although Fowler claimed success, Leader Williams, then engineer of the Bridgewater canal where the experiments were tried, disagreed and reverted to steam tugs.

Thirty years before this James Smith, a cotton spinner of Kilmadock, Perthshire, had, under his Patent No. 8238 of 1839, proposed the use of a steam driven wheel-boat, the propulsive force being a wheel running on the canal's bottom. This would, one fears, have had ill-effects upon the clay puddle, and today would be inextricably entangled in the cars, prams, pushbikes, polythene and other rubbish which represents the bottom (and often top) of a waterway.

However, in May 1888, at the suggestion of Frances Webb, one of the finest railway engineers of all times, an experiment utilising narrow (18″) gauge locos was tried on the Middlewich Branch of the Shropshire Union canal. Although successful, inasmuch as four loaded boats were hauled at 7 mph (11¼ kph) without stress, the cost of providing rails and making good the towing path was sufficient to deter further expansion.

In 1914, at a singularly opportune time, in view of the shortage of horses, the North Staffordshire railway, operators of the Trent & Mersey canal introduced electric tugs through Harecastle Tunnel at a cost of 2½p per boat per trip. These tugs were powered by battery boats — recharged each trip — and hauled themselves along a steel cable laid through the tunnel, thus vindicating Fowler's scheme. After the war, an overhead system, akin to that of trams, came into use, remaining a compulsory mode of haulage until 1954. The cleanliness of this sys-

William Symington, designer of the *Charlotte Dundas*, which in 1802 plied the Forth & Clyde Canal

tem, despite the lurid flashes and crackles that accompanied the tug as condensation got between the skate and conductor wire, may be gauged when following a boat fitted with an ill-kept diesel or out-board after going through in the quiet times.

On the long summit pound of the Worcester & Birmingham canal — 14 miles (22½ km) — three tunnels, Tardebigge, Shortwood and Wast Hill, totalling 3919 yds (1195 m) meant tedious delays as boats were legged or (whisper it quietly) shafted through and steam tugs were introduced in 1876. Based at Tardebigge New Wharf, most of the men came from Gloucester and they perforce lived in a large shed at the wharf, returning home as and when rosters allowed. Two years later a row of cottages, still extant, were built, nicknamed, logically, 'Tug-Row'. The first tenants were Frank Rowles, Isaac Bolton, William Hawkins and William Veale, who dealt with Tardebigge and Shortwood tunnels, their colleagues Walter Harries, Fred Botton and Ernest Adkins were housed above Wast Hill tunnel.

Three steam tugs were used, the *'Birmingham'*, *'Worcester'*, and *'Gloucester'*, with the *'Stoke'* built at the company's maintenance yard at Stoke Prior being

Legging

added later. *"With two tugs working and two in reserve, these tug crews worked to a time table, summer months every 2 hours from 4 a.m. to 8 p.m. The tug crew being relieved at 12 mid-day by a fresh crew to work on till 8 or 9 p.m. In the winter months the hours being 6 a.m. to 6 p.m."*. During 1908-9 these steamers were replaced by semi-diesels named 'Birmingham Oil', 'Worcester Oil' and 'Sharpness Oil'. The 'Sharpness' was the only one of the three to have her exhaust coming out under her stern at water line, and when towing a 'heavy' load — 6-12 boats of 32-40 tons each boat — through Wast Hill tunnel, the crew would inhale the fumes. After the crew had been rendered unfit by 'sleepy sickness' twice the tug was withdrawn from this work until later when a gas-engine driven fan in one of the tunnel air-shafts reduced the 'fug'.

The late George Bate, one-time Foreman-Carpenter at Tardebigge, from whose reminiscences these extracts are drawn, recalled that in 1918 he steered a loaded boat through Wast Hill. *"It was household coal for the lengthsmen, lock-keepers, toll clerks, weighbridges, offices, etc., an annual supply in those days. This load we had collected from Mrs. Brockhurst of Ostlers Street Wharf, Birmingham, to be left at Bittell to start the delivery the next day. I was the last and 8th boat on the tow through the tunnel, I had to borrow a tow rope off the tug, there being no rope on the boat strong enough for towing a loaded boat. I had no light, and was I pleased when I got to the other end of the tunnel, I should just say I was"*.

Steam towing, Apperley Bridge, Leeds & Liverpool Canal, 1953

Due to the flow of traffic up the Worcester & Birmingham canal which depended on a ship arriving at Gloucester Docks where she would discharge direct into narrow boats in all haste, congestion often occurred, with unfortunate effects on the capacity of the tugs. T & M Dixons handled ship loads of maize; Scribbons, bakers and confectioners of Smethwick, took wheat while Cadbury Brothers of Bournville would arrange for sugar to be handled by boats of the Severn & Canal Company — and sugar being hydroscopic it had to be got under shelter as soon as possible. *"I remember one morning* (continued George Bate) *in the 1920s there were 8 loaded boats, loaded with sugar for Cadburys, at Tardebigge. The steam tug was preparing to tow these boats through the tunnels at 10 a.m. In the meantime the boats loaded with sugar kept on coming up through the summit lock. By the time the tug started she had 10 loaded boats on tow, or so the skipper, a Mr. William Hawkins, thought, but when they were out of the tunnel [Tardebigge] and going past the Old Wharf, he noticed, on looking back at the tow, that he had 14 loaded boats (all carrying 32 tons of sugar). At the workshops on the New Wharf we maintenance men saw Mr. F. Rowles, the office manager, gesticulating to some of the boatmen not to hang on the tow because the tug had its limit in 12 boats. 'Wait*

The *Compton Queen* at Penkridge, Staffs & Worcs Canal, 1910

for the next. You can't all be unloaded at once' he called, but it seemed they wanted to be all together!".

During the first world war many boatmen volunteered for service and as with most military matters these square pegs, ideally suited for operating the barges that ran behind the front lines in France, were hammered into round holes and served in the Infantry or Artillery. Later both men and horses were requisitioned, never to return, although curiously, injured mules were brought back and ended their days pulling boats, a seemingly cruel practice but we are told *"the mules did get better. Many number ones [independent boat-owners] made a good living by working hard, hardly ever stopping. An old shoe was tied behind the mule to give the illusion of someone walking (this was called backering) and thus wife could sleep while husband worked and vice versa, but mules were not popular and many of them would not obey orders unless given by someone wearing khaki. Some of the boatmen got wise to this and obtained an item of khaki clothing"*.

98

The Defence of the Realm Act, 1914, allowed the control of canals to pass into the hands of the Board of Trade. Railway-owned canals were regulated by the Canal Control Committee from 4th August 1914, but by the end of 1916 many independents who were intially left to go their own way, faced both with spiraling costs and a fall in manpower (from the 8273 of 1914 to 5452 in March 1917), were facing bankruptcy. The Aire & Calder canal alone lost 1300 men, the Bridgewater 260 and the Leeds & Liverpool 350, while tonnage fell from 27 million in 1914 to less than 20 million in the same period. From 1st March 1917 all usable waterways fell into the net giving in the main many advantages. The net revenue was guaranteed to be that of 1913, most employees over 25 were granted protection against the 'call-up' and canal companies' requirements in maintenance materials were given a 'priority certificate' for supplies. *"Men were secured for them from the Transport Workers Battalions and a training school for boatmen was established at Devizes on the Kennet and Avon Canal, where some 200 men of these Battalions*

Traditional working of traditional boats, Trent & Mersey Canal

were given a three weeks' training in canal boat work. These trained men were afterwards posted to canal carriers and companies. The Canal Companies were assisted in dredging and maintaining their waterways and in keeping them open for such traffic as could under the conditions prevailing be diverted to them . . .".

But even this change in status could not alter the fact that on the controlled canals in 1918 there were only 9586 boats at work of which:

        5488 were engaged in coal traffic
        213 were engaged in grain traffic
        667 were engaged in timber traffic
        103 were engaged in provisions traffic
        3115 were engaged in general traffic

with 1076 boats awaiting repair, 159 crew-less and, ominously, 1344 boats idle, this latter including 1000 or so compartment boats on the Aire & Calder canal as the export of coal was greatly reduced due to "the submarine menace".

Contrary to reason, despite vastly increased output from factories, and hence input of raw materials, despite railways being overloaded and road vehicles greatly reduced, canal traffic had suffered a blow from which, with few exceptions, they were not to recover. Statistically the figures are self-explanatory.

TONNAGE CONVEYED ON SOME CONTROLLED CANALS

Canal	Length Miles	1913 tons	1916 tons	1917 tons	1918 tons
Aire & Calder Navigation	85	3,597,921	2,095,290	1,866,750	1,594,441
Birmingham	159	7,090,628	6,601,755	6,449,201	6,091,735
Bridgewater	52	2,171,311	1,618,470	1,508,296	1,355,961
Glamorganshire	35	374,398	248,981	206,664	242,693
Gloucester & Berkeley ⎤ Worcester & Birmingham ⎦	55	363,924	304,273	251,843	240,426
Leeds & Liverpool	145	2,308,210	2,185,127	2,054,552	1,899,701
Rochdale	34	512,061	291,415	366,364	354,266
Staffs & Worcs	52	722,876	535,799	476,675	487,123
Weaver Navigation	20	1,138,643	876,496	743,737	668,348

The grand total showed a fall from 27,059,908 tons transported over 1221 miles in 1913 to 18,816,994 over the same mileage in 1918. Reflecting the cost of living, wages of employees rose astronomically between 1913 and 1919. Sample figures will suffice:

Trade	Pre-war wage	1919	New demands, 1920
Toll Clerks	£1.39	£3.25	£4.45
Boatmen	£1.19	£3.02	£4.33
Lock-keepers	£1.10	£2.75	£3.95
Foremen	£1.77	£3.88	£5.08
Tug-Captains	£1.57	£3.22	£4.50
Blacksmiths	£1.51	£3.58	£4.75
Carpenters	£1.45	£3.26	£4.75
Dredgers	£1.16	£3.00	£4.75
Labourers	£1.06	£2.71	£3.91
Painters	£1.50	£3.15	£4.75

These figures were, of course, based on a nominal 48 hour week for boat-handling personnel, and 47 hours for maintenance men. To make matters worse in 1920 *"the men are seeking for all public holidays on full pay and six days holiday per annum with pay; the provision of clothing for boatmen and other special allowances"*.

In 1917 there had been one of the worst frosts known on the system, which caused stoppages of up to six weeks from late in January to early March *"and this at a period when anything that interfered with or interrupted navigation on the canals was nothing short of a national disaster in view of the fact that the exigencies of the great war were straining our resources to the very utmost, and war stores of every kind were vital, if our armies in the field were to but hold their own"*. With the cut-back in man-power, ice-boats were unable to clear the track and eventually the army were called in to assist but even so this frost materially added to the worries of the canal companies. Not so the boatmen, he had to be philosophical for *"once the canals are allowed to become ice-bound, they are absolutely impervious to the hottest language, and one can only sit and think, and occasionally use language, until the thaw comes!"*

So there were the three factors, falling trade, rising costs and weather, which bedevilled and to some extent destroyed waterways; one at a time they could cope with, three at once — no! The first important casualty was the carrying fleet on the Shropshire Union canals. When the Canal Boats Act was introduced in 1877 certain restrictions were placed upon the number/age/sex of the occupants of 'cabin', or living, boats, roughly requiring that each adult was to have 60 cubic feet of pure air space and children under 12, 40 cubic feet, with separate accommodation to be provided for children between 5 and 18 years of age. Oddly excluding Scotland, this Act further stipulated certain ventilation requirements.

To enforce this and later Acts the Shropshire Union canal had by 1903 employed a 'Lady Inspector', but a side-effect of the Acts was a fall in the number of family boats (as opposed to those with an all male crew) and following the

An incredibly diabolical device under the guidance of its inventor enters the bottom lock of the Bentley Canal, c.1917

war the number fell even further; in 1902 there were 450 boats, in 1920, 202. It was not therefore a great surprise when the LNWR, as owners of the Shropshire Union canal, faced with demands for parity in wages and hours with railwaymen, announced with regret that on and from 1st September 1921 they proposed to withdraw the companies fleet "though until further notice the Waterway will be maintained in the hope that the Public will make use of it by their own or hired Boats on payment of toll". Some, probably not more than half of the fleet, were taken over by bye-traders, mills, ironworks and other firms. 'Railway' boats, i.e. those owned by the LNWR (later LMS) serving as feeders from railway depots to canalside works and power stations, although declining in number, continued to function until 1950, the Docks & Inland Waterways Executive still operating a fleet of 60 or so within the Birmingham Canal Navigations for a further four years.

Even in the period 1917-1925 various 'improvements' in boat propulsion were propounded including one by an aerial wire ropeway manufacturers who rightly claimed that *"nothing really useful will be accomplished until the present old-fashioned method of hauling barges along canals by means of horses is scrapped and done away with entirely"*. However, they went on to mention that *"towing by steam propeller boats does considerable damage to the banks and bottom of the canal, owing to the wash of the propellers"*, also true. Their method, which has, one feels, a familiar ring about it was that haulage *"would be by means of endless continuous haulage ropes running backwards and forwards in either direction"*. In detail, though, they claimed one hundred tons pull could easily be generated, using ropes in lengths of about 7 to 10 miles each with automatic connection from one to the other, *"with driving power stations, each station serving two sections, spaced 14 to 20 miles apart, depending upon the amount of traffic and the nature of the country, etc. We have a special form of gripper, by which the boats to be towed would be attached on to this endless hauling rope by means of short lengths of two ropes, a connection between the tow rope and the haulage rope being made by means of the special gripper*

Traditional cargo still operated. Tom Humphries (left) and Archie Dove loading barrels of lime juice at Brentford Depot, Grand Union Canal

New works on the Grand Union Canal

already referred to, in such a manner that the speed of the boat is entirely under the control of the boatman whilst remaining in his boat". The hauling ropes would be erected on each side of the canal on steel posts, *"so as to be entirely out of the way of the towpath"*, and which they stated would not interfere in any way with ordinary horse or tug haulage. One wonders what happened when the boatman let go in order to pass or be passed by another boat? Trying to re-hitch would call for great dexterity and, one suspects, much profanity! Still it was a brave try, although never reaching more than the theoretical stage.

One incredibly diabolical device was brought into use and, thankfully for the boatman's sake, just as quickly forgotten. This, the brainchild of a carrier, T.H. Coggins of Coggins & Arthur, was named the "Hooke Patent Detachable Power Unit" and, briefly, consisted of a four-cylindered "Marine Internal Combustion Engine" bolted onto a bed-plate which in turn was bolted to the top of the cabin. In 1920 internal combustion engines were not the finely engineered, utterly reliable, peacefully quiet, machines of today but in addition to their noise, vibration, fumes and petrol lurking in front of the boatman, transmission at roughly waist level was by means of an exposed "horizontal telescopic shaft" which through gears drove a primitive outboard or z-leg arrangement. It did however, have an electric (magneto) starter. Its designer (not entirely modestly) stated, *"I feel I am on quite safe ground when I claim that as a speeder up of canal transport there is no device at present in existence that can touch it"*. Various examples were cited to prove its efficiency, among them one of rather dubious veracity: *"perhaps the very best testimony that can be advanced in regard to the general utility and reliability of the Hooke detachable motor is the fact that our own War Office have employed them most successfully for military use on the French canals in the war zones"*. Another, on February 28th, 1918, involved taking two empty 'dumb' boats plus a 'motor' from Smethwick to Hednesford Coal Basins, in all 28¼ miles (45 km) in 6¾ hours, bringing the two loaded boats back in 10 hours, which was not unreasonable. One claim, though, does not stand too well, that an empty boat did the journey from London to Birmingham in 50 hours, 20 minutes, *"beating the best known record by 10 hours"*.

A steam cargo carrying fleet of boats appeared on narrow canals as early as 1864, when the Grand Junction Canal Company purchased the *Dart* and others, although a decade later these were purchased by Fellows, Morton & Clayton. Prior to the first world war, using a four-man crew spread over the steamer and its butty, an average time of 52 hours was normal between London (City Road Basin) and Birmingham (Fazeley Street). Working was extensive, by 1912 terminal points included not only Birmingham but Leicester and Nottingham. Despite a reasonably economic power unit and the glorious silence that always accompanies steam, the lost space both for engine and fuel meant that various other experiments were also carried out, including Thornycroft and Crossley gas motors, British Kromhout heavy oil engines and, towards the end of the war, Gardner semi-diesels. Eventually, however, the order for new engines went to the Bolinder Company, boats being re-equipped between 1912 and 1924. The last ex-FMC steamer in normal service was damaged beyond repair in 1931 after sinking in Hillmorton Locks on the Oxford canal.

On the Leeds & Liverpool canal where the need to conserve space was not so vital, steamers ran from 1880 until the mid-1950s although not until the last twenty years or so numerically superseding horse-drawn boats. Unusually, this company forsook horizontal 'Scotch' boilers for vertical ones, feeding four-cylinder compound engines, non-condensing. In 1894 in service on the Leeds & Liverpool canal were to be found a mere 26 steamers, with the canal company owning, in addition, 130 horse-drawn boats; 894 horse-drawn craft were operated, or at least registered as operational, by bye-traders. In 1921, as a mirror to the Shropshire Union canal, carrying by the company ceased. Subsequently a number of traders fitted their boats with the locally-built single cylinder Widdop semi-diesel, but rather oddly the last commercial working boat of the old pattern (sugar ex-Leeds) to pass over the summit in 1960 was horse-drawn; although odd runs by diesel boats have subsequently taken place, as did the local coal run to Wigan Power Station.

After the formation of the Grand Union Canal Carrying Company in 1929, which brought together the constituent parts of the long runs between London & Birmingham and Leicester & Nottingham, the company thought to rebuild the old main line, Braunston-Birmingham, where the single narrow locks led to uneconomic working — and it was hoped not only would pairs of narrow boats work through from London to Birmingham, but also wide-beam barges with a minimum capacity of 55 tons. In parallel with today's grants, whereby unemployed people on 'make-work' jobs have their wages met by the Government, albeit now entirely on restoration schemes or other 'amenity' projects, men were taken off the dole and given work. The grant, however, only allowed for the widening of locks and bank retention work, not for the planned widening of bridges or modifications to the underwater profile of the canal, this proving to be the Achilles Heel of the big barges as they spent more time getting 'hung-up' (stranded) on corners than progressing. Incidentally, after using Kromhout and Bolinder engines, the Grand Union Canal Carrying Company again turned to

Horse-drawn barges on the Regents Canal, 1954

the continent, using in the barge *Progress* a Junkers diesel, the sound was a fore-runner of much to come.

However for their fleet equipment programme, the Company settled for (almost entirely) the use of National diesels, but placed their orders for motor narrow boats with two separate companies, Harland & Woolf of Woolwich and Yarwood of Northwich. Although both were issued with dimensional outlines, their working drawings were quite different. The motor boats also came in three sizes, with varying constructional details, some being 'composite' — steel sides, wood bottoms — others all steel. The unpowered 'butties' had much the same complications, with the additional one that some were entirely wooden, being built by Walkers of Rickmansworth.

Together with older, experimental, boats there was shown on the fleet list of the Grand Union Canal Carrying Company a maximum of 386 boats, including the oddity *Acturus,* carefully, having regard to boatmen's feelings, numbered 12A. This fleet, or so hopes ran, would give the GUCCC a virtual monopoly of carriage, and by means of their boat control system, introduced in the late 1930s, enable the craft to run on a timetable. At very least, the Controller would know where any boat was at any given time; thus when demand exceeded supply unladen craft could be diverted to the collieries, docks, etc., while laden craft, assuming for example they had on board boiler fuel, could provide a rapid supply to whichever works required it, thus, hopefully, avoiding the time lost queueing to load or discharge. As a corollary, the use of road vehicles to carry goods urgently needed would be eliminated, or at least reduced.

It might have worked although companies like Fellows, Morton & Clayton were also expanding; but for it to work the men were needed, the men who were not there as we can tell from the 1939 Annual Report of the GUCCC. *"Once again throughout the year the company has suffered from the lack of skilled boatmen, which seriously handicapped its operations, and in consequence many thousands of tons of goods were lost"*.

One obvious result of the expansion of motorised craft was a continuous decline in long-distance horse-drawn craft, although of course, even on modern waterways like the Regents canal running through London, they still found extensive use but for shorthaul journeys only. On this waterway the horses, or rather their drivers, ran into a lot of trouble at one time and another. Feeling the horse strain against the obstructions in the canal — and these horses were drag-ging a weight in excess of 75 tons — the driver would crack his whip, a crack that could be heard above a quarter of a mile away. Some, undoubtedly well-meaning, do-gooder hearing this would 'phone the canal company head-quar-ters and complain bitterly, telling a tragic story — with embellishments — of how this horse was being flogged. Almost invariably investigation would elicit the truth, that the whip-crack was a signal to the nearest lock-keeper to tell him the water was low in the pound.

9
THE AGE OF SHIPS

When by means of outright purchase or lease a railway took over a waterway they inherited certain obligations as well as advantages.

The network of waterways that made up the Shropshire Union was a diverse selection of oddments including the Ellesmere (opened in stages 1795-1833), Chester (1779), Birmingham & Liverpool Junction (1835), Montgomeryshire (1797-1821), Shrewsbury (1796) and Shropshire (1792). They had at various times merged with one another until the whole was brought together as the Shropshire Union Railway & Canal Company in 1846, with grandiose ideas of a massive rail network derived from, and in part incorporating, their waterways. The LNWR, not altogether approving of the plans of this rival, offered and had accepted, lease terms in 1847.

The LNWR had as its Chairman the redoubtable Richard Moon, whose instructions to all his servants, including those on waterways, laid down a standard from which, alas, we are far gone. *"Remember, first, that you are a gentleman; remember, next, that you are a North Western Officer, and that whatever you promise you must perform — therefore, be careful what you promise, but having promised it, take care you perform it".*

Following this precept, the Shropshire Union was worked efficiently and every possible traffic source was sought; to the disgust of the GWR who had almost a total rail monopoly of that area.

Among other minor characteristics was a sensible scheme for investing modest amounts of money in the hope that the traffic engendered might justify the outlay. One which didn't pay but which was a very nasty thorn in the Great Western and Cambrian Railway Companies hides was the Glyn Valley Tramroad whose origin went back to 1799 when the Ellesmere canal reached Chirk and theoretically opened up markets within Shropshire, Cheshire, and even Birmingham and London for the slate mines in the Ceiriog valley. It took a further 74 years before the quarry owners, the Cambrian Slate Company, and the local landowners were to have other than packhorses to transport their products.

In 1872 the Shropshire Union Railway & Canal Company — already shifting 40,000 tons of coal, limestone and slate annually from the area — agreed to provide £5,000, half of the capital required to build an 'economy' tramroad.

Steam had already arrived on the Birmingham & Liverpool Junction canal

Shropshire Union Canal. Transhipment point from Glynn Valley tranroad (note rails and horse-dung) c.1906

where steam tugs towed trains of narrow boats, but on the tramway it was considered horse traction (at about £1 per animal per week) was cheaper. A curiosity was the passenger carriage attached to trains as and when required, inasmuch as this was a 'toastrack', where rows of seats stretched across the body, open above the waist — hardly suitable for winter travel in Welsh Wales!

Traffics consisted of slate, granite, timber, coal, tiles, bricks, lime and 'market produce', mostly transhipped to canal boats although some went to the GWR for onward shipment by rail. However, losses more or less consistent at £750 p.a., became the order of the day and after attempts to introduce steam traction in 1878/9 the Shropshire Union Railway & Canal Company sold its interest in the tramway at a loss of £2,630, the transfer becoming law in 1881. The total loss, including operating losses, of the tramroad to the canal company (or rather the LNWR) was in excess of £7,000, but of course they had gained canal tolls — and aggrieved the GWR!

It must be understood that a canal cannot be — as one still hears wished — just 'closed'. Given enough excuse, whether on political, economic or engineering grounds, they can be 'closed to traffic'. Even today this still happens for main-

Ellesmere Port, November 1920. Salt Union Ltd. barge towing three flats. In the foreground the steam tug *Bridgewater* is towing a sailing vessel bound for Runcorn

tenance purposes, when a waterway, nationalised or privately owned, can be closed 'until further notice'.

Logically, therefore, the best way to close a canal to traffic is to carry out minimal repairs, as low in fact as is consistent with safety. Having established the bank works are weak, the pound levels between lock flights have to be lowered — which reduces the payload carried by the boats, which cuts back traffic and so on ad infinitum. On the other hand, if the canal is useful to the holding company then an adequate water supply is essential. An unusual and little known aspect of canal engineering is the means of supply and, as important, the regulation of water. Basic sources are many including, for the long term, rivers, streams and reservoirs, but up to 50% of all canal water may come by way of land drainage and surface catchment which, naturally, alters levels very quickly and for many years the waterway engineers have endeavoured to calculate this inflow. One way is by means of rain gauges of which the basic components are a funnel and a retaining vessel, which vessel is decanted into a specially graduated glass and the results then read off.

The Peak Forest, Macclesfield and Ashton canals passed into the hands of the Manchester, Sheffield & Lincolnshire railway in 1846 and the railway company's canal department maintained no less than 35 of these gauges well dispersed throughout the system; the one at Manchester being the busiest! The location of the gauges was vital as they must not lie in a position where wind currents are affected by buildings or trees, and to aid the plotting of flow patterns the heights

110

of locations varied from 16' (5 m) to 1669' (509 m) above sea level. The 'General Instructions to the Officers and Servants' issued by the railway company in January 1863 laid down the procedures involved:

"At stations where there are rain gauges, the water collected in these gauges must be carefully measured, and the measure registered in the book provided for that purpose. This must be done every morning, as near eight o'clock as practicable; a weekly return being sent to the Canal Manager. The fall of water taken each morning at 8 a.m. must be registered as having fallen on the previous day. In the case of frost or snow, the bottles must be thawed every morning".

A useful income to any canal concern was always to be derived from the sale of water to factories or (initially) to other canal companies. Domestic supply was also arranged, normally via a reservoir and filter beds — the going rate paid by Manchester in 1848, drawing from the Peak Forest canal was 0.83p per 1,000 gallons. Private persons wishing to draw water paid 25p and farmers between £2 and £5 per annum.

A rather unusual use for canal water was to drive mill-wheels; in most circumstances the fall of water was insufficient to give the necessary power, although one way was to use the overflow weir normally found above a lock to fill a mini-reservoir behind a pen-stock, the water after use exhausting via a leat to below the tail of the lock.

Water-powered cranes, hoists, winches and other winding gear were to be found in many canalside buildings, the water being fed via a culvert. Such a water operated crane was once to be found at Great Bridge canal/railway inter-

Macclesfield Canal, Bosley locks, 1950

Ashton Canal, 1969 — Dukinfield

change basins on the Birmingham Canal Navigations. Here railway trucks laden with coal ran along rails raised at a higher level than the waterway, the loaded boats then working to factories which were geared, by reason of their boiler location or inaccessibility to railway lines, to waterside supplies. There were, however, hazards involved — at least in the 1840s.

"*The sidings adjoining the Canal basin gave us a lesson in Station Yard working. They were laid unavoidably on falling gradients, and in spite of warnings and cautionary notices, again and again the wooden stop blocks at the end were broken up and wagons went into the Canal. A heavy stone buffer block suffered the same fate, and Mr. McClean's resident Engineer, Mr. Walker, determined to try the effect of dispensing with buffer stops of any kind; the danger of careless running of wagons was patent to the shunters, and there followed a perfect immunity from such occurrences* — the danger ensured the safety!*"*.

The LNWR claimed, rightly or wrongly, that their rail traffic between Liverpool and Manchester could in no way be said to make a profit; but by 1882, faced with the certainty that Manchester, as a trading city, would continue to decline, for the city had never really recovered from the American civil war which cut off supplies of cotton and was strangled by the port dues charged by Liverpool (it was claimed that even in 1852 of the total charge to transport a ton of goods to Calcutta — 96p in 1881 — 61½p was expended before the vessel left Liverpool), Daniel Adamson arranged for a meeting to consider two possible schemes for a

Sir E. Leader-Williams, designer of the Manchester Ship Canal

Irlam locks — masonry, gate skeletons and overflow sluices all under construction c.1892, Manchester Ship Canal

Queen Victoria on board the Royal Yacht *Enchantress*, towed across the Canal immediately prior to the official opening in May 1894 — Manchester Ship Canal

Ship Canal. The first, tidal, projected by Mr. Hamilton Fulton was rejected, mainly on the grounds that at low tide only the masts of vessels would be level with the quays, but a second incorporating five changes of level and drawn up by Mr. (later Sir) E. Leader Williams was accepted as was his estimate of £6,309,536 (excluding purchase of land) for completion. Subscriptions were raised and after some struggle on 6th August 1885 Royal Assent was given for the works to commence.

By early 1887 though, the canal must have been seen as a tantalising mirage, for a first attempt to sell shares to the public failed, as did a prospectus placed on the market by Rothschild's bank. A change of Chairman from Sir Daniel Adamson to Lord Egerton of Tatton in mid-1887 appeared to clear the air and by 4th August a further prospectus had led to the raising of the minimum capital required.

The first sod was cut by the Earl of Tatton on 11th November of that year and although (typical of any canal!) prices rose, and the contractor died half-way through the works, the opening for trade took place on 1st January 1894, Her Majesty Queen Victoria formally opening the works on 21st May 1894.

Between 1894 and 1899 the tonnage shifted on the canal rose from 925,659 to 2,778,108 and receipts in proportion and on 16th January 1899, the SS *Manchester City* arrived from St. John, New Brunswick, with 7,500 tons of cargo within her length of 461' and beam of 52'. Just like her forbears on the Bridgewater canal she carried a magnificent mixture of goods, including 450 head of cattle; 150 sheep, 469 packages of poultry; 1,416 boxes of butter; 11,972 boxes of cheese; 37,117 bushels and 1,500 bags of oats; 67,000 bushels of maize; 39,919 bushels of wheat;

Steam tug towing three tugs past Manisty Mount, near Eastham, after the opening of the Manchester Ship Canal, 1894

3,408 bales of hay; 6,470 bundles of wood pulp; 1,000 sacks of oatmeal; 1,084 cases of eggs; 1,250 tierces of lard; 4,600 bags of starch; 500 bags of sugar; 246 standards of deals and ends; 4,274 doors; 245 bundles of doors . . . and a variety of smaller parcels.

Since then, of course, the Manchester Ship Canal, following the path laid down by Adamson and Leader Williams, has consistently been developed to meet the new requirements of trade; by 1909 it was necessary to increase the depth of water from 26′ (8 m) by 2′; this was achieved not by dredging, as this would be of little avail, the lock sills against which the gates abut being the governing factor, but by raising the water levels. Four years (13th July 1905) before this, No. 9 Dock — some half-a-mile in length — was opened by their Majesties King Edward VII and Queen Alexandra; at the head of which was to be built in 1915 the No. 2 grain elevator, in its time the largest of its type in the world. With a storage capacity of 40,000 tons overcrowding was unknown and barges did not have to wait long for their loads!

During the 19th century the bulk of oil products arrived in casks, but after a

Barton aqueduct, c.1760

certain German gentleman had persuaded a motor vehicle to throb into life, demand grew and at Stanlow, near Ellesmere Port, work began in 1916 on building oil refineries and their depots, the first being opened in July 1922 but such was the growth of demand that eleven years later a second dock, doubling capacity and handling facilities, was completed.

Unfortunately, the Manchester Ship canal by its very existence physically eliminated both the Mersey and Irwell navigations and the original Barton Aqueduct — that 'Castle in the Sky'. Jeremiahs of 1760 forecast it would fall, their prophecies took 130 years to come true! The original proposal for its replacement was to carry the Bridgewater canal over the Ship canal by a high level aqueduct, lifts — similar to Anderton — raising and lowering boats from the canal. When this was shown to be unrealistic in terms of both labour costs and mechanical complexity, Leader Williams metaphorically rolled up his sleeves and designed that 'Wonder of the Waterways' Barton Swing Aqueduct. Hydraulically powered it is — even now — as much a marvel as Brindley's old aqueduct was, for its overall length is 235' (72 m) and swung weight (including water) is no less than 1450 tons. Opened to traffic on 21st August 1893 it remains more or less

116

unaltered today. Notwithstanding this, the tonnage moving along the Bridge-water canal fell slowly, although just under two million tons were still moved annually prior to the first world war; after this the growth of road traffic had an ill effect — it will be remembered that vast numbers of ex W.D. lorries were disposed of cheaply, giving traders, with little capital outlay compared with barges, more than competitive rates. Tonnage was halved by 1923 and down to 366,000 tons by 1952, this despite attempts at modernising the waterway.

The future for this, the first 'main-line' canal in England, seems, as with too many waterways, to lie in pleasure craft; a curious contrast with its successor!

10 THE AGE OF AUSTERITY

Although the inter-war period had caused the disuse or closure of some water-ways including inter alia the Bradford (1922), Droitwich Junction (1928), Pock-lington (1932), Thames & Severn (1933), Leven (1935), Manchester, Bolton & Bury (1936), Grantham (1936), Montgomery (1936), Nottingham (1937) and Shrewsbury (1939), some canal concerns had recovered to the trade levels of pre-1914; the Aire & Calder for example was carrying around 2½ million tons, how-beit rather quaintly, alongside the newest 'pans' running back and forth, loaded and discharged mechanically, still plodded a dozen or so horse-drawn barges, functioning as they had done a century or more before. The war brought much to a grinding halt, with maintenance once again the sufferer.

Although canal men could, if they so wished, be regarded as in a 'reserved' industry, nevertheless many volunteered. On some waterways the jobs of the men had been kept open during the slump of the 1930s, but two or three-day working had been the norm, with the obvious results on family finances. Odd though it may sound, during the 'phoney war' period the armed services appeared to offer greater financial security.

During the inter-war period too, on many canals, work had been kept at a min-imum level. The Shropshire Union Canal management now in the ownership of the London, Midland & Scottish railway, faced with a fall in tonnage from the 433,000 of 1929 to 151,000 in 1940, was glad enough not to bother with bank repairs or much else and under an Act of 1944 around 100 miles of the network were abandoned for navigation purposes leaving only the old main line and the Welsh branch still in use; the latter being regarded at that time as a vital drinking-water supply channel.

The extent of falling traffics on waterways may be typified by one example, the Worcester & Birmingham (including the Droitwich canals) where tonnages fell from, in 1931, 135,000 via 120,000 in 1936 to 60,000 in 1941.

One problem found today on maintenance is that not many apprentices were taken on during the two decades of falling traffic 1930-1950, and the leeway has not been made up. Just what we have lost is all too apparent. Looking down the stoppage programme for Worcester & Birmingham canal the average time allowed to fit new gates is 14 days, by comparison the late George Bate writing about the 1930s claimed:

Decline of traffic. Derelict boats on Rochdale Canal

"When I had made a new top end gate I would never ask the inspector, Mr. E. Spiers, for a stoppage to fix the gate in the lock [but instead] after I had taken a new top gate down the locks to where the old gate was to be replaced, I would, the next morning, make enquiries by 'phone first at Birmingham and then Worcester and find out where the traffic was and I would calculate the time it would reach the affected lock. If the times were suitable I would get my mates to erect the shear legs and change the gates, put the stop planks in and start to fit the new gate up to the quoins and clap sill before the trade came to where we were working. I had worked this method with new top gate fixing and fitting from the 1930s up to 1965 [never more than] one day and one day to realign the clap sill if this should be necessary. The men I usually required were 5 or 6 labourers or lock-keepers. It is only since taking lock-keepers away from the flights of locks that locks have become fouled up with mud and debris taking 2 or 3 hours to clear away before you can get to work at the gate or gates, indeed on some bottom end stoppages it can take a day to clear out debris before work can commence on gates and sills".

Even in the hard times of the 1930s when you worked there were compensations; George Bate again — only this time in humorous vein. "I saw one woman go in the canal at Whitford bridge. She was pushing the gate with the shaft and went head-first into the water. The boatman saw it, rushed back and pulled her out, pulled the boat back under the bridge-hole but he wouldn't let her go in the cabin to undress — no! he was houseproud! — and he handed the clothes out to her. And I said to her after, 'That was a bit crude wasn't it?'. And she said, 'I've undressed before better men than thee' and I said, 'Well anyway it would be worth looking at a second time!".

119

'Volunteer girls'. Note lack of ornament on boat and the pushbike for lock-wheeling

John Knill's motor *Columba* — well laden

But what pride that couple had in their boat! And how in that period, and the decade after the war, boat-people worked — and at best only scratched a living. One result of the stress and strain of that rough boating was that although marital ties between the boatman and his wife were rarely broken they came under some tension. It happened one day that a gas-oil boat of Thomas Clayton (Oldbury) was working up the eleven locks at Aston on the Birmingham Canal Navigations when the butty steerer accidentally let the helm slip over and broke the tiller. The husband was that wild he threw his windlass at her, *"He 'it 'er on the shoulder, so of course they had a row all the way up the eleven [locks] then they were arguing about how they were going to steer the bloody boat. They struggled and mauled and got the boat to the top lock and then they came to me and I fixed them up with a bit of old timber that I shaped into something to fit the tiller to get them back to Oldbury.*

"Then three days later old Danny's arguing with her and got his fingers in the strap [towing line] and lost the end of two fingers. It didn't stop him from going to work. Bloody 'ell, you'd got to have your 'ead off in them days to stop boating".

Perhaps it was the lack of this toughness that made the volunteer girls who crewed a few boats during the war appear so conspicuous. With the sole exception of one crew who 'made good' they were regarded by boatmen with some amusement, and it is to be feared that in some cases they were only playing. Eily Gayford who supervised their training, and who was to receive an MBE for her

121

work, found some were not strong enough and others had to leave *"because of their parents"*. And commercial boating was hard graft, quite different from today's 'pleasure'. It is pleasant enough, even at 5 a.m. — providing no hangover is present — to amble along at the tiller of a boat in summer, but in winter hazards are present which can make even the most experienced of crews worry. Over a Christmas recently two of the crew of three, while engaged in ice-breaking broke an extra hole in the ice with their bodies, one at a top gate as the lock was filling and the day after that the second man fell over the fore-end of the boat. Luckily the boat was deflected by the ice or else he would have been run over. Small wonder that while many boatmen might look back wistfully at their summer days, having learned to drive in the army, on a winter's day they were glad to be behind the wheel of a lorry.

One minor resurgence of traffic occurred shortly after the war, when a few ex-officers, unwilling to conform to the mores of 'civilisation', used their gratuities to purchase one or more boats. Most survived for a while ekeing out their earnings with such money as they had left but the growth of trade unions was against them, as dockers, reasonably enough, bearing in mind their position in a dying industry, gave preference to the card-carrying boatmen, and after 1948 to their fellow employees within the Docks & Inland Waterways Executive. At the beginning of 1947 on the Grand Union canal alone a wide variety of carriers was to be seen, many of these boats working elsewhere as and when required.

These carriers included the Grand Union Canal Carrying Company and Fellows, Morton & Clayton plus A. Wander & Co., whose 'Ovaltine' boats were kept particularly smart; S.E. Barlow of Tamworth, coal carriers, whose long dis-

Traditionally decorated, the new butty awaits her launching

One of the famous Black Warwicks using back-boards to increase her load of coal

tance operation was also primarily to the Ovaltine works; Harvey-Taylor of Aylesbury; Wyvern Shipping; Faulkners; Samuel Barlow; Thomas Clayton of Oldbury and the famous 'Black Warwicks', the Warwickshire Coal Carrying Company, operated by Gilbert Brothers of Charity Dock, Bedworth.

It was probably unfortunate that under the Transport Act of 1947, while railway and road interests were given their own authorities, canals were an unwanted appendage to the docks. The Docks & Inland Waterways Executive which came into being on 1st January 1948, took under their wing 1766 miles of waterway which were suitable for commercial traffic. Their first apparent move, apart from issuing reams of paper, was to paint their boats in blue and gold, eventually eliminating boatmen's individual touches such as had been present on the GUCCC boats, a blanket effect heightened when Fellows, Morton & Clayton almost immediately abandoned carrying.

However, even in 1950, 11,802,000 tons of cargo were still shifted, half being of coal products, the other including oil, flour and grain, metals, cement, sand, pottery materials, paper, chemicals, timber, sugar, wool and agricultural products. The fleet — and bear in mind this included not only canals but estuaries — totalled some 130 power or dumb barges, 650 compartment boats and roughly 400 motor or butty narrow boats. The D & IWE claimed, "All possible steps are taken to ensure that inland waterways, in co-operation with the railways and roads, make their full contribution to the national transport system and that the public will derive the utmost benefit from an efficient and economical service".

As they saw it the only parts of the system worth mentioning by name were

123

A pair of Willow Wren Canal Carrying Company's boats travelling breasted up along the Grand Union Canal, Braunston, 1963

the Humber, Mersey, Thames and Severn estuaries and the Aire & Calder, Regents and Gloucester & Berkeley canals, together with the Lee and Stort rivers. 'Subsidiary routes' included Ellesmere Port to Wolverhampton (i.e. the old Shropshire Union) and Manchester to Stoke-on-Trent or Burton-on-Trent (i.e. the Trent & Mersey). *"The canals in the Birmingham area"* said an official handout, *"provide connections with the other [D & IEW] divisions"*. Succinct, but sad. For Scotland, the Caledonian *"afforded a safe and convenient passage for trawlers, tankers, tugs and barges . . . [and] is of particular appeal to tourists . . . apart from commercial craft, in summer the canal is a favourite haunt for yachts and cabin cruisers"*. Similar impressions, with the emphasis on pleasure craft, were recorded of the Crinan, Forth & Clyde and Union canals. Welsh canals might have been erased for the space they got!

These quotations are drawn from a blurb of 1951, in which *inter alia*, the Forth & Clyde was said to provide *"a safe efficient and easy route between the East and West coasts"*. In 1955, 171 pleasure craft, 15 cargo vessels and 119 fishing boats worked through the 39 locks and 35 miles and in the following year 139, 14 and 98 respectively passed. A year later it was doomed, due to the progress of the Denny bypass on the Glasgow to Stirling Road, which would have required some expenditure on a lifting bridge and so for a mere £160,000 a canal which cost about half-a-million pounds to build was scrapped, the coup-de-grace being given by the 'Forth & Clyde (Extinguishment of Rights of Navigation) Act 1962'.

The Kennet & Avon although physically in being was totally ignored, the craft dimension table showing the depth of water as 18″ (46 cm) with "sections closed for repair" — a situation which remains today.

The performance of the D & IWE where maintenance was concerned was

Beautifully decorated, a pair of Samuel Barlow boats lie at rest, 1951

Bascote 2-rise locks, Grand Union Canal 1949

The Monmouthshire Canal in a state of decay

curiously mixed, for example, in 1952 three very smart new diesel tugs, *Naseby,*
Olton and *Selby* were delivered for use on the Regents canal, but the same year the
Steam Flyboat No.38 was the last boat to pass Hurst Lock on the Barnsley canal.
Two years later they were playing with an air-propelled boat, new storm paddles were fitted to Bittell Reservoir and, pessimistically, the 'safety gates' which
isolate sections of a waterway, were overhauled on the Worcester & Birmingham canal. Dredging works, including new boats — which for the Leeds &
Liverpool canal were delivered by road — were going on at a great pace, yet on
the Birmingham Canal Navigations, although the locks were in poor condition,
'make-do-and-mend' was a normal practice. Stan Turner, the then carpenter
and part-time lock-keeper on the Aston Flight tells how this problem could be
exacerbated.

  "Little Jimmy and Ernie, they left Oldbury about quarter to twelve one night and came
down, it would be about two o'clock when they went through the tenth lock of Aston. When-
ever I heard a boat that early going down I always used to get out of bed and have a look through
the window. There was only gas light in the house in them days but it was light enough for me
to see the name of the boat or to see whichever one of the boatmen appeared. With that I went
back to bed and about quarter to four there is a banging on the door and it was Violet Beach, she
said 'I'm in a bit of trouble down at the bottom lock'. I said 'Why?' and she replied 'I've just
gone to push the bottom gate open and I've pushed the beam off'. I said, 'Well, you'm a strong
wench then, it takes eight blokes to put them on!'. I went down to the bottom lock, the balance-
beam was on the floor, the head was still fastened to the head of the gate but the other end was
on the floor. So I did no more but said 'Got a torch in the boat?'. They got a torch out and I just

126

shone it and had a look and there, right in the middle of the beam, was a lovely big dent and when I looked at the heel the tennon had just literally disintegrated straight off. As Jimmy Beach was there I said, 'Come on Jim' and we wrestled this beam and got it back up on the heel of the gate. I borrowed some rope off him and roped it back up into the collar hole and tied it there so that we could work the gate. I said, 'There's one [boat] gone down in front of you isn't there? Jimmy and Ernie?'. He said 'Ah' and I said, 'Any more coming down?'. He says 'No'. I said 'Alright, I'll have it fixed for when you come back'. Gets on me bike and went to Icknield Port and got a cramp, we used to have a special cramp [and other pieces] that held the beam on as a temporary measure. I waited for Jimmy and Ernie to come back and I said 'How did you get out the bottom lock this morning then?'. 'Opened the gate and went out'. I said, 'Who put the bloody beam back on the gate for you then?'. They argued blind with me, I said 'Come here, let's have a look' and there right on the front end of the boat were the splinters from the beam. They forgot that! Then they told me, they whipped up three paddles, Jim had got the [check] strap and he strapped but it [the strap] broke and instead of hitting the beam just off centre they hit it smack centre, so it had got to go''. 'Strapping', i.e. dropping a line over the head of the gate, was the normal method of stopping a boat — but it could be hard on the gates!

Boat lying in a dewatered pound

During their period of control, roughly 6 years, the D & IWE claimed to have spent in all a whole two million pounds sterling on maintenance and when from 1955 the canals were hived off under the 1954 Transport Act to become British Transport Waterways (in effect a satellite of British Railways) officialdom was able to work off some of the spleen that had built up as a result of the pushing and prodding of such bodies as the Inland Waterways Association and Inland Waterways Protection Society who had thwarted various canal closure attempts. Aside from the main estuaries and the small ship canals (the Manchester Ship canal had avoided nationalisation) the bulk of the waterways were regarded, officially, as being *"in such a poor state millions [of pounds] would have been needed to make them commercially navigable"*. Note the past tense was already in use — in October 1955! As waterways contributed less than 0.5% of the turnover and staff of the British Transport Commission (the overall directors of nationalised road, rail and canal interests) their influence on transport events was negligible, as indeed it remains today. The Inland Waterways Association had, by this time, published their scheme for a National Waterways Conservancy which would be an entirely independent body *"empowered to operate and promote them [waterways] in all their functions including trade, pleasure boating, industrial and domestic water supply, angling and housing afloat . . . [and to] positively and vigorously exploit all their constructive possibilities, commercial and other, in the world of today . . ."*. Alas for the dreams we have lost!

As time went on virtually all independent carriers went out of business, to some extent due to natural wastage — there was not really much point in replacing boats when the trade or even the canal they ran on might be eliminated, and to a lesser extent due to the changeover of factories from coal to oil firing. As senility of the canals, boats and attitudes of mind took its toll so the weight fell more and more upon the shoulders of the lower echelons. Stan Turner again, still at Aston:

"My Uncle was a lock-keeper with me, we did two shifts and he was on afternoons and he was putting his locks right at night about 9 o'clock and it was dark then and he was always a bit timid, and he asked me to go to the bottom lock but I was just ready to go out so I said 'Bloody well go down yourself, take your torch with you, you won't hurt nothing'. So he goes to the bottom lock, but never took his torch. When he got down there the lock gate was open so he just shut the lock gate without looking round. Arthur Roads had brought a loaded boat up through the lock into the pound above but the wind had blown the boat back into the lock, and my Uncle shut the gate without seeing the boat. Well this lock used to leak itself empty when the top gate was shut and the boat was right up against the top gate and being a very slow leaking lock the boat quietly went down until the thimble [which held the rudder] of the boat got onto the bumper plate, and once it lodged there as the lock emptied the stern end of the boat just went down into the canal and sunk. At 2.30 on the Saturday morning there was a terrific bang on my door and somebody shouting 'Where the bloody 'ell are yer?'. I got out of bed and put my head through the window and looked and it was Mac and he says 'I can't get in the lock, the gate's fouled'. So we sent down and took the bottom end rake. I said, 'You got a torch?'. He said

A land based dredger scoops up thick mud

'Yes'. We shone it in the lock and he weren't likely to open the gate because there was a bloody sunken boat there, sitting with its nose up on the cill and its cabin on the bottom, loaded with 26 ton of coal. I went to the 'phone and 'phoned Dick Holt [Superintendent] and told him no boats could go through because this was sunk and I had to change the trade around from one place to another, and while I was away Mr. Roads who was manager for Walkers [carriers] came to have a look at it and whips three paddles up and washes it off the cill so that it was lying flat in the bottom. Everybody thought it was marvellous because it was lying there looking as if we were going to get it up easy and we fetched the stop-planks and put them in and brought the two pumps, went to start them and they wouldn't go. British Waterways pumps you see, and they wouldn't work! So John Wright's fire brigade promptly offered their services with nice brand new pumps and none of them would go! So the firemen all promptly got the sack! So eventually we went and fetched another couple of pumps and pumped the lock out. There was an old fellow there, a fifty-odd year service man, who said 'All we got to do now is fill the lock and she'll float'. Although I told them it wouldn't they wouldn't believe me. They filled the lock and the boat still stayed sunk. So then Stanley [the narrator] had to empty the boat by throwing all the nuts [coal] out onto the top of the lock, all 26 ton of it! Then we found out that the back of the boat was broken with a gap of about 9″ between the bottom boards and the side, which we promptly put about 8 to 10 ton of clay along and made a stank [watertight barrier] and put two 2″ pumps on the boat and having floated it took it to Saltley Dock with the

129

pumps still working, had all the schoolkids bowhauling it down the towpath like race-horses".
Bowhauling is pulling by ropes: there was no engine on this type of boat.

In 1965 overall tonnage fell to 7.9 million, with only 5% carried on narrow canals the working deficit on the system stood at £625,000. Economies were achieved in many ways including keeping lock gate renewals to a minimum, using lighter and cheaper forms of bank protection, eliminating lock-keeping and, the most salient factor of all, manpower working on the length was reduced from 4343 (1962) to 3432 (1963). Under Section 64 of the 1962 Transport Act the British Waterways Board had been permitted to maintain all their navigations at the same (low) level as existed during the six months preceeding 2nd November 1961 — a year later they congratulated themselves on having this 'moratorium' extended for a further year!

So far down were our canals that we thought there surely was no way but up.

11

THE AGE OF THE CRUISEWAY

'Restoration' is, to modern canal enthusiasts, an evocative word, conjuring up visions of boundless Government aid, unlimited people-power and an endless succession of waterways which, overnight, shall be made available for amenity — but never commercial — use. It is all the more anomolous that few of the maintenance men employed by the British Waterways Board, show more than a passing interest in such matters.

To some extent this is probably caused by human nature — having just completed 40, 45 or 50 hours work on the canal often in very poor, if not downright atrocious conditions, that is enough. Many are married men with families and to an increasing number of BWB personnel waterways are no longer a way of life, but just a job.

Only a few years ago a breach occurred on one of the midland canals. After a week or so, rather to the amazement of the BWB men working on the job — a singularly tedious one mainly involving throwing bricks out of the bed of the canal via a human chain — the local canal society, not noted for its enthusiasm in getting their collective hands dirty, offered to assist at the weekend. A dozen or so duly turned up, beautifully dressed in clean, pressed, slacks, white shirts and yachting caps, and after their Commodore had given his orders, commenced work — not cleaning up the canal, but instead gathering up all the scrap brass and copper lying about. When the BWB men could get over their shock at seeing all their lovely 'tat' disappearing they asked "What the tut-tut was going on?" "Oh," said the Commodore, disarmingly, "we thought we would sell this and be able to buy the paint to tidy up our wharf".

In general the methods still in use by the British Waterways Board for the maintenance of the track are the manual-orientated ones of their forbears. Reasons are simple — there simply never has been the money available to invest in mechanical plant which would probably be under utilised, that labour is still cheap — there is a running battle between farm labourers and BWB employees as to who is to be the lower paid — and given the nature of most country canals unless the item is portable enough to be brought by a boat most of the waterway will be inaccessible. To quote a fairly common occurrence; a rathole is made in a bank, this develops and becomes a leak. The ditch at the back of the bank is probably long overgrown, forgotten, or has been ploughed up by a careless tractor

Maintenance works

Leak prevention. New piling near Brandwood tunnel, Stratford Canal, being back-filled

driver. The hedge if not grown into a jungle will have a good layer of bottles, beer cans and fishermen's impedimenta at its foot, all of which reduces the chance of the local length-foreman seeing the leak as he makes his monthly patrol. When the field is nicely flooded the farmer will 'phone up the Section Inspector (perhaps incidentally making a claim for a damaged crop) who will have to decide which of his gangs can be withdrawn from another job — one told me that suspended animation would be the only answer to his manpower problems — and whether the hole is accessible by road. If it is not which boat can be made available? This type of boat can make a vast difference to the speed of the job as some are incapable of being fitted with a motor and theoretically, at least, each man must not bowhaul (pull manually) a loaded boat for a greater distance than one mile (1.6 km), thus a three man gang will not, in practice, be able to cover more than 5 miles (8 km) within a normal working day. If no 'tump' or stock of clay is conveniently placed for the job when can it be delivered and to where? Incidentally, to circumvent the sluggish paperwork machinery most Section Inspectors wisely keep an order for a load of clay, sand and gravel and cement in hand, ready processed, but without delivery instructions. By the time these factors have been sorted out the foreman should have visited the site and will know the applicable degree of urgency.

133

Volunteer Length Persons take a rest on a balance beam, Long Lees lock, Calder & Hebble Canal

All leaks are urgent — especially after the calamitous breaches that have occurred over the last few years — but some are more urgent than others; where the bank is built on greensand it would receive quicker treatment than in an area where piling has taken place or a strong retaining wall is still *in situ*.

The problems resolved, the gang, probably dragged off a nice warm hedge-laying job, will glumly survey the area, reviewing the foreman's instructions which in all probability will be happily and necessarily vague. It is axiomatic that the leak half-way down a bank started life 20 or more feet (7 m) away and, due to saturation of the bank, will have been reinforced by a multitude of smaller snivels. Rather oddly, older men always formally describe the magnitude of the waterflow in plumbers terms i.e. ½", 1", 2" pipe, although amongst themselves the descriptive venacular, piddling, pissing and pelting are more common!

A hole, or more likely a series of holes dug and the leak (hopefully) traced, clay is trodden in the resulting excavation, 3" deep layers at a time. The process of fettling can be mechanical, but is more likely carried out by big Wellington

Hire boats c.1900 — advertisement

A hotel conversion of a butty boat — the quietest way to travel

boots. Judging the right amount of water for the process requires the eye of
experience, ideally it should be just heavy enough *"to tear the sole off yer boot"*.

Because of their habit of only tackling large jobs, few volunteers have experience of this work, but one good service to the BWB is carried out on a few canals
by "Volunteer Length Persons", men and women who 'adopt' a mile of waterway and regularly patrol this, reporting any defects to the local foreman. Obviously a weekly patrol over one mile even by an amateur is better than a monthly
patrol over the 15 miles (24 km) or so that a BWB foreman may have to cover.

The main problem besetting most 'cruiseways', i.e. waterways used primarily
or wholly by pleasure craft, is that the original depth of water is rarely attain-
able, and where it is a vicious circle is set up. Too many pleasure craft are grossly
over-powered, weighing, perhaps, 7-9 tons they appear to need the same 30-40
bhp engine as an 80-ton barge. This is often to compensate for a poor hull design,
but also it is true that hirers are growing more adventurous and need these large
engines to make headway against the Trent or Severn in flood! But having this
power and finding deep water the hirer accelerates, forcing the boat through the
water and causing an immense wash plus undertow. Anyone standing on the sea-
side will be aware of the abrasive effect of an ebbing tide — canal banks face this

136

Hire boats of the 1970s

action 100 or more times a day — and naturally enough the soil of the banks caves in. Not only does this silt up the channel but weakens the root-grip of the trees along the bank, which were once, long ago, planted to retain and consolidate the self same soil! As dredging proceeds by means of a mechanical digger, in itself a slow process, the spoil is boated away but due to speeding boats that deeper water is silted up behind the dredger, imperceptibly at first, but within a period varying between one and five years the work of the men will be negated.

While linear dredging is the most satisfactory, its very slowness may mean that bridges become impassable further along the canal and have either to be cleansed manually or that the dredger will have to do a 'tip-and-run' exercise cleaning out bad places, then returning to normal duty. Disposal of dredged material is becoming more difficult, and much time is lost getting to and from the tip. Where piling or camp-shedding has taken place this can be backfilled with mud from the canal. This piling, normally using interlocking lengths of con-

137

"All right, start talking!"

"Extra lorry trips will be necessary"

voluted steel, will stand proud of the bank by 3′ (1 m) and unfortunately, unless great care is taken, the removal of the mud can weaken the hold of the piles, and they are in time undermined.

Generally, restoration workers rely upon hired plant (although they own much, often secondhand) but save for the odd steam or lightweight diesel dredger, land based draglines are preferred, usually capable of working along a towpath. Hired lorries then transport the mud to suitable tips. Of course BWB use draglines and restoration groups dredgers, but the primary differences between the two methods is that a dragline gives a V shaped channel due to the scooping action, while a water-based dredger can follow the original U profile. The second, non-technical, difference is in manpower, BWB use (on average) 4 men; 2 tug drivers, 1 dredger and 1 discharger operator but restoration groups (working over a shorter period) can use a dozen or so men and women.

One very noticeable change in the approach to maintenance work occurs geographically. In the North-East and the London area, where commercial traffic still has precedence, time is important, and such primitive equipment as the manually lifted 175 lb (79 kg) air-hammer used in the Midlands for piling is super-

138

Today's scenery. Ocker Hill Power Station, Walsall

seded by boat-mounted machines, the latter having quadrupled output with far less physical effort. It is not at all coincidental that North-Eastern waterway officials have nicknamed the Midlands area 'sleepy hollow'!

In 1975 the British Waterways Board went 'into the red' by £8 million, but while 954 persons were employed in administration the labour force had dropped to 2262 (from 3432 in 1963) of whom only 1438 worked on the canal banks — roughly one man to each 1.67 miles.

Pleasure (amenity) waterways incurred a deficit of £5,965,200 — an impossible £209 loss for each craft on the system.

Canal cruising has always been the preserve of the reasonably well off, but never more so than today. In many ways boat-hirers have suffered the worst, for the rise in weekly hire costs is prodigious; only a decade ago £20 was an adequate fee for a six-berth boat, fitted with chemical toilet, evaporative cooler and two rings plus grill for cooking. Primitive perhaps, but it was fun with helpful boat-yards and placid lock-keepers to help you on your way. Propulsion was by means of an easily-changed outboard engine — and more often than not the first five gallons of petrol were free — as a goodwill gesture. A typical six-berth today

139

will have superb fittings including television, refrigerator, full-sized cooker and flush toilet, but such peace as may still be found will in all too many cases be destroyed by the location of the diesel engine. While eliminating the chore of fetching fuel, the bulk of these, to give increased cabin capacity, are located under the steerers' feet subjecting the hirer to a nice steady vibration . . . and a damnable racket. For this pleasure the cost was £187 in 1976 and £209 in 1977. Out of the peak season canals still have much to offer, but in the hurly-burly of summer boating tempers often fray, lock-keepers rapidly disappear and the latest menace, 'cowboys', take a fiendish delight in roaring past violently rocking the boat just as a meal is served, or at 2 a.m.!

One reason for present high hire-costs is that many boats today are operated under an investment scheme whereby the boatyard is commissioned by an individual to build a boat at the market price; this boat, however, being identical in all but minor points with, say, six others. This craft will then be hired out, the owner usually having the use of it for two weeks in the summer plus (almost) unlimited cruising out of season, but the hire fee is split a 40/60, 50/50 or 60/40 per cent basis with the boatbuilder. Until recently adverts in the boating press claimed that 'investment boats' were the answer to financiers' dreams, offering both a good income and at the end of the boat's hire-life — 4 or 5 years — it would be saleable at vast profit. In the January 1977 issue of *Waterways World*, the leading canal magazine in the UK, Mr. G.W. Baker, a director of Anglo-Welsh Narrow Boats, one of the oldest and most respected hire-boat groups, put the matter in its true perspective. *"I have recently seen advertisements in the national press offering for sale new canal boats for subsequent lease to hire companies. In these advertisements the words 'appreciating asset' have been used. I think it should be made clear to all contemplating entering into such a scheme that a canal hire boat is now quite definitely not an appreciating asset, whether in real or money terms. Its rate of depreciation will vary depending on the quality of its construction and the standard of maintenance of the hire fleet to which it is leased, but it certainly will not be less than 12% per year and could well be over 20%".*

It would seem the halcyon days of having profit both ways, in hire and subsequent sale, have gone; indeed a number of boat builders and hirers have disappeared in the last few years, particularly those with heavy overdrafts and hence high interest payments. It is also a little sad to have to record that most of the small, pleasant, companies of the fifties have gone out of business, often as a dumb protest against the brashness of modern canal business methods.

How much more traffic amenity canals can stand, both physically, with deterioration of the track, and in terms of water supplies, quantitively, and numerically, as every boat needs moorings and services, is open to debate.

Worse, though, for all of us, was that in 1975 the BWB Freight Services Division incurred a loss of £116,000. A trifling amount, true, but this was the first loss for over a decade. Spending on motorways by H.M. Government increases yearly but, also in 1975, they turned down a scheme to modernise the Sheffield &

The Caldon Canal 1974

South Yorkshire canal. Costed (1975) at £3.8 million, this plan would have enabled 400-ton Euro-barges to work from the Humber as far as Rotherport — a new shipping complex at Rotherham — but rejection may well mean that within 5-10 years all commercial carrying on this waterway will cease.

So in lieu of the 1.45 million tons going by boat, 48,000 extra lorry trips will be necessary, and against the 54,000 gallons of diesel oil boats would have used, 181,000 gallons more will have to be imported. By building the new barges in Britain we could reduce shipyard subsidies and, of course, the engines could be British.

A final problem facing waterways and their users — not only boat-people but pedestrians on towpaths and even 'gongoozlers' gazing idly at the waterside scene — is one of a changing environment. One perforce accepts that the Government will order the construction of motorways, erasure of charming old buildings and the replacement of homely cottages with 'tower-blocks' or ant-heaps. This treatment is meeted out to waterways as a matter of course, but why is it, seemingly, encouraged by their guardians, the British Waterways Board? They seem to positively enjoy 're-development' schemes — without showing the delicate touch that waterways call for. Mown grass, tarmac footpaths, neat copings along the waters' edge, look smart — but so does a hospital ward or a funeral par-

141

lour. The Board has an architect sympathetic to canal requirements and imaginative schemes are within its scope, but whether any enthusiasm is dissipated before it reaches the men who do the job or is stultified by a lack of finance, the end result is sterility.

It is true that we can walk past city monstrosities, shudder and go on our way, but even in the country the whole waterside environment is being progressively destroyed. The most common birds are — or were — herons, kingfishers, swans and moorhens. The former are doomed to be shot by bailiffs hired by fishing interests; the blue flash of the kingfishers is an attraction to shotgun-toting farm-hands; swans must regard stoning as the norm, and moorhens are sitting targets for youths with air-guns. The poor old moorhen is in fact the unluckiest inhabitant of canals — in not-too-far-off days her eggs were taken by boat and length-men alike, to go with their bacon; then she faced oil-pollution; and now the wash of power boats and the use of steel piles for bank retention is forcing her to nest in trees and sometimes even on the bank. The speed of passing boats too, will disperse her family when they are chicks, so that they are either drawn under the boat or, lost, become rats' food.

Sprays used either for weed-reduction or carelessly sprayed by tractor-drivers must, in time, by dispersal through the water, lead to sterility among all water-birds. The flowers that once graced our canal banks are disappearing fast — mainly through spraying — and, not unsurprisingly, rising costs for hedge-laying means the BWB, like farmers, prefer to replace these with posts and barbed wire. It is the avowed dream of many middle-level waterway officers to eliminate trees, as their removal would reduce maintenance outgoings — it is sad to hear envy in a speaker's voice when referring to one area which has no hedges at all.

With luck, planning officers, by declaring some lengths of waterway as conservation areas, and even occasionally checking the British Waterways Board in some of its more nefarious schemes, may keep some parts of the canal system as attractive 'green fingers'. But, however much we may dislike the thought, the choice for the future of waterways lies entirely in our hands. Shall they all be used for amenity, at great expense to their users and requiring an enormous subsidy from taxpayers? Commercial traffic could still pay dividends both financially and environmentally, but only if funds for investment in modern canals and their crafts are made available; the alternative — all goods by road — will cause even the most apathetic to shudder! Do we really want sterile canals, sprayed and treated, bereft of charm and wildlife? Or should we try to fossilize them — a 2,000 mile linear museum, animated solely by an artificial heart? Which?

12

THE AGE OF RESTORATION

Today's canal scene is really the result of the cold, hard, winter of 1962/63, when the residue of the once-great carrying fleets that operated on the narrow canals of England were frozen in, wherever they were, for periods of up to fourteen weeks. During this freak of nature, loads of coal, timber, oil and tinned fruit were transferred to road hauliers.

The biggest claim, made even today, against canals, is that they are so slow, for not more than 4 mph is possible even on lockfree pounds. This is totally irrelevant to the large user of any item; — as long as the goods arrive every week or day as required, how long the journey takes does not concern him. A continuous flow was the keynote and it was this regularity that finally failed.

Boats being loaded, remained at the wharfs, and the bulk of those already making their way to their destinations, despite prodigious efforts, had to lie where they were — many in remote rural areas. Boats that were discharging could, after completion, do nothing other than crawl behind the icebreaker to the nearest depot, while those running 'light' back to the collieries suffered most, for an empty boat lacks waterflow to the propeller and many were unable even to get within easy walking distance of a road bridge.

Many boat-people were in some degree of distress for, relying upon coal-fired ranges for heat and cooking, which burn about 10 kg of coal per boat per day, the 2 or 3 cwt normally carried as 'dunnage' did not last long, and they were forced to buy or scrounge fuel at a time when supplies to householders were hard to come by. Drinking water was, for family boats, their Achilles heel — standpipes and domestic supplies alike were frozen and canalside springs had lost their flow even when the frozen turf was shifted.

Once boatmen left their boats, as many did, the chances of the traffic recovering was slight; a problem exacerbated by the necessity of docking boats damaged by the ice.

Whether or not recovery might have been possible will never be known, for the decision was taken by the British Transport Waterways to abandon their fleet, although attempts were made to house and re-employ the men. But being born and bred in a warm, comfortable, cabin 10′ x 7′, few could withstand the change to a bleak, unkempt and unwanted cottage. To typify the problem, consider Albert, who together with his wife and three children was first left to live

143

All Aboard for the Waterways

on his butty (unpowered) boat for some weeks — the motor boat returning empty to the Depot — and then offered a notoriously cold, bleak house, which had had a succession of tenants, and by reason of the cesspit and drinking-water well being foul was condemned by the council as *"unfit for human habitation"*. After such a long lay-off, he had little money and ended up eating, living and sleeping in the front room, this being as much as he could afford to heat.

Possibly narrow boat carrying would have dwindled within a few years, faced with the inevitable rundown in the staple traffic, coal, due to the increasing use of natural gas and oil for heating purposes, but who knows? If nothing else canals are resilient.

In 1967 a sudden plethora of headlines appeared in the daily press, "All Aboard for the Waterways"; "Go-cruising Boost"; "Holiday Charter for the Canals", etc., and a new era began, an era of pleasure boating. Some call it 'prostitution of a great heritage', some a logical corollary of the great increase in leisure time; to many people it has given openings to explore their countryside and to some, for-

144

"The Last Coal Run" — leaving Cassiobury top lock 1970

tunately only a few, a means of getting from one bar to another without fear of the breathalyser. Finally for those wise or wealthy enough it was an opportunity of making a quick and easy profit by means of a clever investment.

Parallel with this had come a vast growth in the use of volunteer labour to restore and even operate waterways that a decade or two ago had been written off as only suitable for infilling or 'erasure'. The restoration movement had its roots planted before the Second World War and indeed the formation of the Inland Waterways Association in 1946 provided a *raison d'etre* for all the early enthusiasts. The original 'object' of the IWA was *"to advocate the use, maintenance and development of the inland waterways of the British Isles and in particular to advocate and promote the restoration to good order, and maintenance to good order, of every navigable waterway by both commercial and pleasure traffic"*. While the strength — numerically and financially — of the IWA gives it the power to tackle the Government, its remoteness has led to the foundation of local societies.

The strength of a local society is, simply, that by concentrating its effort on one waterway they are able to approach the British Waterways Board, Local Council and other interests at ground roots level. Some groups, the Birmingham Canal Navigation Society to quote one example, have a heavy but compact mileage of waterways — in this case 159, excluding factory arms and short branches, either in use or possibly restorable — or they may have a relatively short linear track which only requires 'fettling-up' — the Calder & Hebble is in full working order, but members of their society assist BWB workmen by undertaking towpath work.

Elsewhere there still remains a strong feeling of geographical unity, and nowhere is this more apparant than in that amorphous area, East Anglia. While the Great Ouse Restoration Society, River Stour Restoration Society, etc., work upon their own 'patch', all are allied to, and often their members are also members of, the East Anglian Waterways Association, which, unlike some more raucous societies, pursues an erudite but forceful campaign not only for the restoration of some waterways but is unashamedly against 'Broads-type' pollution of its area.

In all there are some 50-60 societies, geographically as far apart as Sussex and Glasgow, varying from the enthusiastic to the supine. Of the many good societies that could be chosen, due to lack of space it has only proved possible to highlight the following five; variety is the keynote.

One of the oldest of all is the Kennet & Avon Canal Trust, founded in 1963 as a successor to the Kennet & Avon Canal Association. This latter had sprung into life in 1951 shortly after the Reading-Newbury section of the waterway was closed by the Docks & Inland Waterways Executive. In 1955 the British Transport Commission attempted to close the canal — largely on the grounds that there wasn't any traffic, but found hitherto unknown opposition. Rebuffed by Parliament, largely as a result of the representations of the K & A.C.A., the British Transport Commission chose instead to let the whole waterway run down, no doubt hoping those canal enthusiasts would go away.

Far from this happening, the K & A.C.T. is a well-organised body with 5,000+ members but having 86½ miles (139 km) and 106 locks to keep an eye on along their route from its junction with the River Kennet at Reading to Bath, central control would be too unwieldy and they possess nine divisions — six geographical, Bath & Bristol, West Wilts (Bradford-on-Avon), Devizes & Pewsey, Hungerford, Newbury and Reading — with a head office for administration, a Youth Division and the Crofton Society who have restored and run the famous steam-pumps.

The Youth Division may well represent the K & A Trustees of the future and logically they have adopted the Caen Hill (Devizes) flight of locks for their 'scene'. Work so far has covered removal and burning of the old gates, clearing trees from the lock walls and chambers and — using a narrow-gauge railway — cleansing and re-watering the top side-pounds (reservoirs). Most are school children and/or Scouts, many of whom camp out on-site, although permanent quarters are provided for use in inclement conditions.

Some 60 miles and 43 locks were navigable or under active restoration by the end of 1976 but despite this considerable amounts of money and unlimited labour are still necessary for its complete restoration.

Although the income of the K & A.C.T. is high, £55,901 being handled in 1975, of which £33,649 was raised within the Trust, the balance coming from special appeals and local government grants, so is expenditure; in the same year £50,825 went towards restoration works. The 1977 figures, suggest an all-round increase, necessitated by rising costs, with a hoped-for expenditure of £108,000 and, regrettably, a shortfall of £17,000. The most unfortunate part of this saga is that, as restoration costs are accelerating so local government grants have to be cut back, thus putting a heavier burden on members' pockets. However, out of adversity good can come as unemployment in 1976 led to the Government, through their Manpower Services Commission, offering to pay the cost of labour on one and, in future, possibly more schemes, the Trust having to find the cost of materials.

The stretch of the Kennet & Avon canal covered by this 'Job Creation' project was a length of 3,117 yards (2,850 m) between Avoncliffe Aqueduct and Limpley Stoke Bridge, where the bed is porous colite and has since the inception of the waterway defied all attempts at puddling. The basis of the new works costed at

Stemmed up

some £238,300, lies in the use of a pervious layer of stone allowing the springs to vent underneath a polythene and cement channel. This completed, the K & A.C.T. 'only' have to ponder on the derelict 29 lock Caen Hill flight at Devizes. This they are determined to restore to its former glory.

This is, of course, a British Waterways Board-owned canal and it is only recently that volunteers have been allowed to undertake other than manual tasks; Bull's Lock, rebuilt to the BWB standard, was completed at about one-third of the 'professional' cost, a saving to both the Board and Local Councils who subscribed the bulk of the funds involved. The satisfaction, or sense of achievement, felt by the volunteers is immeasurable in financial terms.

By way of contrast with the Kennet & Avon, the Pocklington canal has no great centres of population to draw upon and was never in any sense an arterial waterway, but is one of the most Northerly outposts of the one-time network and (shades of Dr. Beeching) was a true 'withered arm' of the railway age. Opened in 1818, trade declined steadily from 1846 when the iron rails reached Pocklington. In the words of Sheila Nix, Secretary of the Pocklington Canal Amenity Society, *"A few keels lingered into the early 'thirties; occasional pleasure boats came visiting; the anglers persevered; the wildlife flourished. But the nine locks were falling derelict, the swing bridges creaked, and the upper sections had long since silted up. By 1934 all navigation had ceased"*.

In 1959 the Sheffield Corporation had the bright idea of extracting water from the River Derwent and depositing the 'de-activated sludge' in the canal, thereby filling it in — over an estimated 30 year period. Pocklington was not so remote that Yorkshire men and women would tolerate that, and as the result of pressure in the local press, a proposal by British Transport Waterways to close the canal was hastily dropped.

In 1968, a local farmer, E.A. Lount, now Chairman of the Pocklington Canal Amenity Society, was fired with a vision of the Pocklington canal clear of weed and mud, once more carrying boats.

The Society was officially inaugurated on 1st January 1969 *"to restore the canal fully to navigation and as a linear country park for all to enjoy"*. An engineering survey was carried out in 1969 by the society's Honorary Consulting Engineer, Dr. C.T.G. Boucher, who estimated the cost of restoration as £44,000. The original cost of the canal, 151 years before, had only been £32,000 — thus have times changed!

A year after their foundation the PCAS, having obtained permission from the British Waterways Board to commence work, organised some 40 volunteers to tackle trees, shrubs, barbed wire and other rubbish above Thornton Lock. Since then achievements, if not spectacular, have been steady.

Cottingwith (1971) and Gardham (1975) locks were rebuilt by the British Waterways Board — the PCAS meeting a proportion of the cost and labour — and the four distinctive brick arched bridges on the waterway were scheduled as

Private owner motor boat *Jaguar* and Company butty *Achilles*

'Ancient Monuments', having, of course, been threatened with destruction at the behest of motorists.

One snag with the Pocklington, as with the Kennet & Avon, is the presence of low-level swing bridges, all of which were somewhat decrepit, but by the end of 1976 four (of eight) had been replaced by new steel-decked ones of a pattern similar to those in use on the Leeds & Liverpool canal.

1976 brought more problems, not the least a revised quotation by the British Waterways Board of at least £84,000 to complete the 7½ miles (12 km) and four locks from the entrance to Coates Lock. Almost simultaneously came the gloomy news that Humberside County Council had, unavoidably, to defer paying for at least a year their promised contribution of £23,000 towards the work. *"Even more frustrating, are the current effects of official work restrictions which sadly hamper both the Board and the Society in arranging voluntary work. Many want fervently today to work with their hands on a satisfying constructive job. The work itself may well be as restorative to them as the finished results. On a Remainder canal like this one, volunteers are unlikely to deprive men of a livelihood. Indeed maintenance, once the canal is restored and upgraded, may well provide extra work"*. Unfortunately the BWB men are well aware of their poor wages (£38.50 a week in 1977) and the lack of recruitment resulting from this and poor working conditions.

Despite these and other problems the PCAS through its magazine *Double Nine*, is still cheerfully optimistic. 1977 saw volunteers working at Canal Head to provide a picnic site where members of the public can enjoy themselves. Further plans call for restoration of the warehouse, lockhouse and the top lock, permission having been granted by both Unions and BWB for the manufacture of working lock gates, — although with a proviso that they must not be used for navigation!

One of the pleasant things about this Society is that although they like money, nevertheless they are not above asking for more mundane items. In 1976, during the drought, the Government suggested that putting a brick in the cistern worked wonders in saving water; *Double Nine* asked its readers at the end of the year not to waste time but *"get it [the brick] wrapped in that nice Christmas paper and get it posted forthwith . . . do let us have any bricks you can muster, any number from ones to wagon loads!"*.

The Ashby-de-la-Zouch canal is another rurally-located waterway and one that was only marginally profitable for the promoters but carrying very high tonnages. The great majority of traffic was coal but through traffic, which included lime, bricks, stone and chippings, even iron and pottery, was always encouraged by the presence of an extensive tramroad network at the top end, and save for a stop lock (with a fall of 1″) at Marston Junction, had a lockfree run throughout its 30 miles (48 km)

Falling into the hands of the Midland Railway in 1846, traffic declined gently. Curiously, its very lifeblood, coal, caused abandonment, by subsidence of the

Audlen locks, Shropshire Union Canal, October 1976

lengths from Moira to Donisthorpe in 1944 and Donisthorpe to Illot's Wharf in 1957.

In 1966, faced with the abandonment threat to a further length, Illot's Wharf to Snarestone, which would truncate the waterway to 21 miles (34 km), the Ashby Canal Preservation Association was founded. This was, and is, probably the only society which owes much to anglers, in this case it was the Measham Angling Association which led the way by calling the original protest meeting. They were, in the upshot, too late to prevent this closure, and with it the last coal run of the Willow Wren Canal Transport Services, who were then operating the famous 'Croxley' run to Dickenson's paper mill. The Birmingham & Midland Canal Company (themselves only formed in March 1965) were persuaded to take over the route, initially from Market Bosworth Wharf and then from Gopsal Wharf which the society (their title by now shortened to Ashby Canal Association) had leased from the Crown. Gopsal was, however, in very poor condition but after many letters from the A.C.A. to virtually every body of any importance and to Members of Parliament, the National Coal Board was badgered into disgorging £1,000 towards the cost of road and wharf improvements. The A.C.A. President, T. Lisney, gave the remaining £400 required and the wharf came into use, albeit for only a short period.

Tom Henshaw of the A.C.A. Committee, summed up the situation facing them in the summer of 1969: *"Maybe it's the fertiliser washed off the fields that makes the weeds grow in the Ashby Canal, but very soon the canal was choked, the anglers could not get their bait through the weed, pleasure boats gave up in despair. At a gloomy committee meeting three members were 'volunteered' to go to Croxley and try to restart the coal traffic, despite having no boats and no idea what a viable carrying rate was"*.

In the next eighteen months the ACA 'Trading Section' (now Ashby Canal Transport Ltd) moved over 5,000 tons of coal from Gopsal to Croxley but then traffic stopped for all time, the factory turning over to oil-firing. In September 1970 the ACA purchased the quarter-mile of infilled canal bed above Snarestone with the intention of putting up a building for local Youth Clubs. One positive move was persuading the British Waterways Board to put in a water tap at Snarestone (normally the only one usable on the canal!) and in 1973 the ACA put in a slipway to allow the launching of road-transported light-weight Sunday afternoon cruisers.

Two boats are owned by the A.C.A., *Flotsam,* a work-boat used for rubbish clearing mainly by the Hinkley Boat Club who are an integral part of the Association, and the trip boat *Ace* which augments funds by passenger carrying in the evenings, at weekends and at holiday times.

Tom Henshaw again, proving enterprise in all forms is not yet dead on the Cut. *"There is no scope for drastic work parties, but we are trying to improve the towpath and renovate mile posts, etc. One very interesting thing happened [in 1976] when A.C.A. put a metal box at the side of the canal, locked with a B.W.B. 'Loo' lock. This box contained maps and information sheets on the Ashby canal, also a foolproof container for donations etc. During the long, hot summer, many hundreds of maps were collected by passing boaters. . . . We made many new members and had shoals of almost embarrassingly nice letters".*

The Narrow Boat Trust, unlike most other societies, is not directly connected with any one waterway, although they have strong links with Ashby Canal Transport Ltd. It all began spontaneously in a beer tent at the Guildford Rally in 1970 when *"a crowd of bods got together"* and started to discuss the end of commercial canal carrying. The problem at that time was that if cargoes were found no boats were available — and by the time they were the cargoes had gone by road. The Ashby Canal Association was faced with the former and a brilliant thought came into the minds of these men. *"We could get regular traffic if we had the boats, so how about forming a Trust to preserve some boats in working condition?".* So it was done.

It was known that the British Waterways Board had invited tenders for a number of ex-carrying boats (no doubt hoping they would be converted) and the Narrow Boat Trust, after a public meeting, decided to tender for three of these, without much hope of even getting one. They were, to put it mildly, "shocked rigid" when they found their three tenders accepted for the ex-GUCCC motorboats Nos. 102 *Alton* and 156 *Nuneaton* together with the butty No. 351 *Satellite,* at a total cost of £2,500. Not unsurprisingly they had only a tenth of this sum but the I.W.A. and other bodies helped out with loans.

Alton superficially dressed up appeared at the Northampton Rally the following year, raising some cash and thereafter *"working parties were held at Norton Canes until people seemed to start losing interest".* Jim Yates, the boatyard owner had agreed to let the NBT have free moorings but *Nuneaton* was deteriorating and was hauled out of the water. It was *Alton,* once more 'prettied', howbeit virtually by one man who put the final coat of paint on during the run to London, that was used in conjunction with *Chiswick,* loaned to the NBT by her owner, for a film contract which brought in £1,000 thus enabling the NBT to pay off some of the loans.

After some disagreements within the membership the point had been reached where a decision on what to do with the boats had to be made. One proposal from a carrying company was that they should lease the boats for a 20-year minimum period, with extensions if they required, the NBT to have no say in their use, nor, indeed, any financial return, although in exchange the operating company would, at the end of the period, hand them back in full working order. This was seriously considered, but eventually the proposal was abandoned due to disagreement over the length of the lease.

In March 1975 the indecision of the Trust came to an end when the boatyard owner, no doubt tired of seeing the boats lying about unattended, stated he would in future charge £5 a week for moorings; to have kept the same boats on a private moorings would have cost, at that time, £12.60 a week, so it was still a bargain but the accounts were already in the red! The decision was taken to sell *Satel-*

lite, she being in the worst condition of the three and use the sum so raised (£1,250) to rehabilitate *Alton* and to patch *Nuneaton.* To quote from the Narrow Boat Trust News: *"The crux of the matter seemed to be that* Satellite *was a poor buy originally; this being confirmed by the fact that none of the negotiations with carrying companies to renovate the Trust's boats under long-term lease included* Satellite. *Having said this, it must be said that a Narrow Boat Trust without a butty is sadly lacking, and every effort should be given towards acquiring at least one, difficult though that will be".*

Martyn Denney, one of the Trustees, continues *"That autumn I asked Tom Henshaw [of Ashby Canal Carriers] if we could get* Alton *ready for camping next year would you operate her? He agreed and subsequently a sub-committee was set up to renovate* Alton *for camping the following year. The counter was like a colander and she needed considerable work on the bottom. . . . Denis Cooper said he would survey, his fees were £15 for docking and a pound a foot for a full survey with drawings. He offered us half-price, 50p a foot. . . .*

"The survey to hand, the work was offered by tender to a number of boatyards; Canal Transport Services Ltd., Norton Canes, being chosen. The boat went on dock on 1st March 1976 at their yard. Whilst CTS were busy with the plating work, it was up to us to completely reconstruct the cabin. On 13th March with the welding well on the way, and just three weekends to go before Alton *had to be delivered to Stenton [Trent & Mersey Canal] for the beginning of the season, we were able to start work on gunwhale replacement and renewal of cabin frames. CTS finished their contract towards the end of the following week which enabled us to make an early start on the Friday afternoon. By working well into each evening, Sunday night saw the hull wirebrushed and hot-pitched, the cabin shell completed complete with masonite cladding. On Monday, 22nd March,* Alton *was refloated and moved out of the dock.*

"Frantic work saw the cabin completed the following weekend, the last coat of paint being applied at 5 a.m. on the Tuesday! By 8 a.m. the boat was on the move to Stenson, the first trip departing on time. After a generally successful season that autumn a telephone call was received from Ashby Canal Transport offering the chance to use Alton *for her true trade, inasmuch as they could deliver a couple of loads of coal to BWB employees along the River Weaver. Within two weeks of the last camper leaving* Alton *received the first 17 tons of coal in her hold for many a year, being loaded ex-lorry at Norbury. This discharged, a further load was taken on board and delivered."*

It says much for these amateurs that they stuck to their task — unlike true boatmen accustomed to the wide and wild outdoors, most of their days are spent in pleasant centrally-heated offices, car showrooms, airline terminals or hotels, and the shock can be great! Martyn Denney again, *"I spent the next four days dealing with nearly 16 tons of the load, between Hunts and Dutton [locks], and having successfully dodged all manner of coasters and ICI tankers, returned up the Lift first thing Friday morning, feeling very wet (it had been the week of the great end-of-the-summer downpour) and rather the worse for wear — have you ever tried holding a shovel loaded with coal in one hand and the old fertilizer bag you are trying to fill in the other? It takes some getting used to!".*

And next on the agenda is *Nuneaton* and then? Who knows, the Narrow Boat

Trust may yet recapture the atmosphere of the canals heyday with 40 boats waiting impatiently at the top of Atherstone Locks. . . .

The over-riding problem found by local canal societies lies in the availability or otherwise of labour. Many of the younger generation wishing to work upon canals have no particular allegiance to any one waterway but possess a sense of nationwide 'feeling' and are amenable to being taken en bloc to wherever their services are best usable. The greatest 'swarming' was on the Ashton canal in 1968 when a derelict canal became navigable almost overnight.

The overall direction is given by a body succinctly named the Waterway Recovery Group, whose work is best told by quotations from the Birmingham Canal Navigation Society's Yearbook 1976, telling in parable form of their trials and tribulations.

> "Here dwelt in the City of the Cross of Stone, persons of evil disposition, who came secretly by night, to the mighty Waterway which passeth through their midst. And, Lo! they bore with them, their unwanted chattels upon their beasts, and in their chariots, and by sundry other means, and came unto the waterway, saying 'Now will we bring forth a mightly splash from the waters, indeed even unto the midst of the channel', and great was the splash thereof, even as they had prophesied. . . . Then came vessels upon the face of the waters, journeying from afar, with bright emblazonments, and merry crews. And their vessels were various in form, being large, even unto many cubits long, or small and lightly made as a maiden's sleeve. And when they came unto the city, their vessels were halted by the shallowness of the waters, and they spake unto one another, saying 'What has befallen us that we cannot journey on?' And they feared exceeding, saying 'We do not wish to stay in this evil place, for verily, the peoples are of ferocious visage, and their dogs do snarl fiercely at our presence'."

After raking about in the canal, the boatpeople raised the question of dredging with the British Waterways Board who replied, "We are but poor, and lacking in slaves, and cannot help you" and they "also sayeth secretly, unto themselves, 'And this is but a Remainder Waterway and therefore we are not obliged to help'".

The Waterway Recovery Group thereupon decided to do the work themselves and "their leader a man of noble bearing, with great moustachios, and a headgear of denim . . . cried out in a voice as of thunder 'Let us go forth even unto the City of the Cross of Stone, and there let us toil as is our custom to bring unto the peoples of that place the pleasures of a mighty waterway thronged with vessels. . . . And while the Sun journeyed across the firmament, they toiled, bringing forth from the waters all manner of vile things which had been cast therein as sacrifice by the citizens of that place. And they piled them into a mighty pile many cubits in length and width, for great was the number thereof. And the citizens came by and marvelled at what they saw, and sayeth, one to another 'What manner of men are these, that toil so mightily to bring forth these things from the waters?'. And they laughed exceeding saying, 'Verily, only those of feeble mind would spend themselves thus'. And they went on their way, much amused."

After this the WRG Samaritans went off and had a drink. "And then came the *night, and the citizens of the city came, and wondered at the mighty mound. . . . and threw the Bloody Lot back in!!!".*

And so the canal world rolls round, on the one hand men and women, whatever their reasons, trying to bring waterways back to life — but on the other vandals, financial interests, the vicious and the thoughtless and the apathetic, trying to destroy our heritage. The future is to be. . . .?

INDEX

157

158